May this book be a blessing
in your life. May you become
Sondrenched and feel Jesus
in the corners of your heart.
You are loved by a
man who died to know you.

[illegible] Heckman

Sondrenched

Sandie Heckman

Scripture quotations used with permission from Joyce Meyer, The Everyday Life Bible: The Power of God's Word for Everyday Living, Amplified Version, 1st Edition. Faith Words, Brentwood, Tennessee, Faith Words, 2009. Permission granted November 2014

WestBow Press books may be ordered through booksellers or by contacting:

WestBow Press
A Division of Thomas Nelson & Zondervan
1663 Liberty Drive
Bloomington, IN 47403
www.westbowpress.com
1 (866) 928-1240

ISBN: 978-1-5127-8314-8 (sc)
ISBN: 978-1-5127-8315-5 (hc)
ISBN: 978-1-5127-8313-1 (e)

Library of Congress Control Number: 2017905848

Print information available on the last page.

WestBow Press rev. date: 05/04/2017

PREFACE

IT'S NOT EASY to live a God driven life. Our world is filled with chaos and noise, and we sometimes become distracted, often missing the tiny love notes that God places on our paths. God. Is. So Good.

One morning, I sat on my porch and Jesus showed up in the sunrise of my life. He painted the most beautiful sunrise to catch my attention. My heart became full, as I found Him between the pinks and blues swirling around in the morning sky. How can a God so big, love so large, and make our heart so full that it seems to overflow? Believe in Him and He'll show you this great love.

For we walk by faith [we regulate our lives and conduct ourselves by our conviction or belief respecting man's relationship to God and divine things, with trust and holy fervor; thus, we walk] not by sight or appearance. II Corinthians 5:7

Day in and day out Jesus pursues our hearts. His love is timeless, and His plan for our lives is unimaginable. Asking Him into your heart is a gift only you can give yourself. This gift of having a relationship with Jesus goes on without end, as it comes with a ticket to heaven. Imagine, as we live our lives here on earth and form this everlasting bond, this loving relationship will continue when we reach His heavenly home.

I started writing short devotionals and prayers three years ago. Writing became an everyday love of mine, as I healed from a total knee replacement. Jesus will meet us at the edge of sunrise, where the sun rises at the edge of a new morning. I found Jesus three years ago on one of my darkest days of healing. A total knee replacement is one of the most painful surgeries, but as I healed Jesus filled a void of loneliness that I had been suffering from. As I lay in my bed in my tiny apartment, Jesus showed up in a heartfelt embrace as the beautiful sunrise streamed through my window. On one of the hardest healing days of my life, Jesus came and I safely tucked Him into my heart. His healing grace washed over me and our relationship began to grow. I grew in my faith as I read the word of God. I started writing the words of my heart, words of devotion to Jesus. Three years ago, I began a writing journey and I soon shared my words with family and friends. I began to realize that these words soothed their souls and gave them great peace. I wanted everyone to know how it felt to have Jesus in their lives.

I started attending a local church in my area. I noticed what a difficult job it can be for a pastor to minister to their congregation and continue to stay focused on their relationship with Jesus Christ. Life happens, and as I watched my pastor's offer up words of encouragement and healing prayers, I truly felt Jesus put this desire on my heart to lift my pastors up with encouraging words.

Seven Days, Seven Texts to my pastors began as a week of texting my pastor's uplifting words of encouragement. Even those who preach the gospel need tiny reminders of Jesus' love. Everyone needs a gentle reminder, a touch of the Son. The more I texted my pastors, the better I felt. I became Sondrenched in blessing others with encouragement. When friends and other church members realized what I was doing, they too wanted to receive these daily texts of uplifting words. More than one hundred people now receive a daily dose of the Son, a daily reminder of Jesus' love nudging us all closer to our Heavenly Father and His Kingdom that awaits us, when we open our hearts to Him.

Sondrenched is my gift to you. My hope is that you find a touch of Jesus on these pages, written with love in my heart for a man who died for you and me. I've discovered that Jesus touches my heart the most at sunrise and sunset. I've grouped some early morning prayers and devotionals into a collaboration called Sonrise. If He meets you in the evening, you'll find readings you can find peace in called Sonset. I hope these words calm your soul as you rise for your day or as you drift off to sleep. Find the fine lines of grace in the sunrises and sunsets of your life. The fine line of red and blue that greet each other at dawn, or at the end of the day as dusk settles in. Jesus will meet you at these fine lines where He'll fill your heart with love. He adores you and wants nothing more than to have a relationship with you. Meet Jesus at the fine lines in your life and become Sondrenched in His love. Jesus is pursuing us daily. He's sending tiny love notes in the form of sunrises, sunsets and in the tiny smiles of your family and friends.

I pray that your love for Jesus will multiply with every word and devotion on these pages. May your love for Jesus extend and develop to its fullest, and may your knowledge of this love provide keen insight and discernment. May you live a God-driven life knowing that someday we will all meet Jesus in Heaven.

Selah

ACKNOWLEDGEMENTS

FOR MY LORD and Savior, who breathed life into me and continues to work miracles in my life each and every day. I raise my hands up to You, and I am in awe of all Your blessings and glory. I will be your prayer warrior until my last breath. Only for You Lord. Your will, your way always.

To my beloved Sarah, my daughter and the love of my life. You are an inspiration to me. I love how you change the lives of children every day. May your life be blessed, and may you know Jesus Christ is the reason.

To my beloved father, Darrell F. Litsinger (01/03/1923 to 11/08/2014). You taught me about Jesus from the minute I was born. I still hear your words of wisdom and faith in every word I write. I love you, Dad!

To Kathryn Hart, even during my darkest hours, you believed in me. You helped plant the seed to finding Christ again! I will forever be grateful to you. Thank you for baptizing me in the name of Jesus, our Lord, and Savior, 05/29/13.

To Eileen Bennett, thank you for putting all the words in the right places and for putting up with my craziness as you helped to edit Sondrenched.

To my Pastors Scott Sutherland and Bradley Williams, thank-you for your words of wisdom, prayers and for sharing your passion for Jesus. Your sermons are forever embedded in my heart.

CONTENTS

Sonrise

I DESPERATELY WANT YOU TO KNOW

I'D RATHER SIT at home writing words on paper that tell you who you are in Christ than wander aimlessly through life writing nothing at all. I often wonder who you are, why you're here. What do you think about yourself and your relationship with God? I know for a fact He loves you. If you question who you are in Christ, hopefully, He's shown you that you are His first love. You are His!

How do I know that He wants you to know His love for you? It's really quite simple. If it weren't for Him dying on the Cross, where would we be? We'd be nowhere. We simply wouldn't be. Jesus loves us more than we know.

So, I'm glad you are here. I'm glad you've found Christ in your heart! I'm glad that you seek for more, more of Him. With such joy for Jesus in my heart, it allows me to draw nearer to Him and feel His love flow through me onto paper.

I hope my words calm your soul and raise your awareness that He loves you like no other. You are His child - your citizenship in Heaven awaits you.

The Lord your God is in the midst of you, a Mighty One, a Savior [Who saves]! He will rejoice over you with joy; He will rest [in silent satisfaction] and in His love He will be silent and make no mention [of past sins, or ever recall them]. He will exult over you with singing. Zephaniah 3:17

YOU ARE A MIRACLE

GOD IS WITHIN us and the spaces in between us.

Divinely guided, let us be the miracle He created us to be.

Inhale His grace, exhale your worries.

We know how God's story ends. He saves and grants us eternal life.

IN THE SONRISE I FIND YOU, LORD

I WOKE THIS morning, Lord, and there You were waiting for me in the dawn's early light. Beautiful as ever is your love for me.

As I rose, I felt your love shine through the sunlight in the morning dew and in the leaves of the trees, dancing gracefully in the gentle breezes of a brand new day. On this day I feel stronger than ever before, and I'm happy knowing that You are here to greet me.

How is it possible that each day You could love me more? How is it possible that as I fall You pick me up higher than ever? There You were carrying me on those misty days, the days I had to endure before I was able to call out your name for your love and guidance.

So, on this new day, as I rise to the dawn's light, I'm brighter and stronger than ever before. I know that you're always waiting for me in the early morning, giving me grace like never before. I awake grateful and with open arms. I wait for your loving embrace in the early morning light.

ALL THINGS ARE POSSIBLE

WHAT'S THIS LOVE that tugs at your heart? What's this feeling you know is right, but sometimes gets pushed aside because life gets busy? Call God closer, closer than ever before. Live your life with the expectancy that all things are possible with God.

He's right there with you, but He wants all of you. Today, let Him in all the way. No turning back. Your future is and can be magnificent with Jesus. Keep His name on your lips and in your heart all day, every day.

Today is His day to be your one and only. He loves you and wants you to love Him totally. Push those things, those bothersome problems into His lap. He's waiting. Today is the day to set yourself free.

HE WILL PROTECT

HE WILL PROTECT you. He'll help you through your trials, but most of all His love will never stop. Pray for His will. Pray to see His beauty in everything. For every prayer, lift up your life to Him. He'll show you the way to a joyful life. Pray to see Him moving in your life.

Father, we ask that you blanket our homes with protection. Protect our children as they go to school and while they're at play. Protect those overseas in our armed forces, and those that choose to protect our cities each and every day. We ask that You watch over our firefighters, police and those who work in hospitals around the world. We ask that You watch over our families and friends as they go about their routines. Keep us safe and shine your brilliant light upon us. Guard our hearts and protect us in our daily lives. Selah

In the reverent and worshipful fear of the Lord there is strong confidence, and His children shall always have a place of refuge. Proverbs 14:26

THE GIFT

MAY YOU WAKE up thankful. Seek joy in all the little things today. Life is a gift. Open it wisely. If you go about your day quickly, rushing here and there you miss so much. You miss the beauty in the sunrise or the spectacular smiles on your loved ones' faces. Life's too short to rush it. You'll get there soon enough.

Slow down the pace, and savor the day. Be mindful of those around you. Smile more, giggle often and realize the cherished moments you can offer others.

Spend a moment, just an extra minute, telling someone they're special. Tell someone they're loved. Hug more. Enjoy today.

Stop being so hard on yourself. Eat ice cream for breakfast, lunch or dinner. Just enjoy today. You deserve it. Tomorrow will come soon enough.

You are a miracle. You woke up breathing. Make someone's day special. Let them know they are a blessing, too. Shine and be your brilliant self.

And He has filled him with the Spirit of God, with ability and wisdom, with intelligence and understanding, and with knowledge and all craftsmanship Exodus 35:31

BE YOURSELF

STRIVE TO BE yourself today. Those who swim against the current usually end up out of breath. Go with the flow – the flow of God. He's molding you, giving you unique purpose.

Giggle often. It reduces wrinkles left from frowns!

Let go today. Allow God's love to flow through you. He's really good at changing situations and lives. He changed the world by giving us His Son.

It is because of the Lord's Mercy and loving-kindness that we are not consumed, because His [tender] compassions fail not. They are new every morning; great and abundant is Your stability and faithfulness. The Lord is my portion or share, says my living being (my inner self); therefore will I hope in Him and wait expectantly for Him Lamentations 3:22–24

CHANGE

SOME PEOPLE SAY when you have Christ in your heart you change. If you're going to change, change in silence. People take notice, and those who are down on themselves will be haters. Let the haters hate, spew their words that you cannot take to heart. Show them who you are in Christ, and how much He loves them. Show those your heart of grace by showing them, love. Change is inevitable in all of us, but when God changes our heart people will notice a change in us. Things won't bother us as much, joy becomes our number one attribute, and our hearts change into love filled chambers that God fills up constantly. Change – be the change that Christ died for, and change our world.

So teach us to number our days that we may get us a heart of wisdom Psalm 90:12

STANDING TALL IN FAITH

I WENT FOR a drive past corn field after corn field. How I love the growing season! I love to see corn growing row after row.

When we're in a season of growing in God, it can sometimes be hard. It reminds me of how corn grows in a field. Each row of corn is precisely planted and standing tall. Plant next to each plant, reaching straight toward God.

When these seasons of growth are upon us, we must stay firmly planted in God. The rows of corn growing so close together remind me of how important it is to have faith followers in our lives, each of us standing together growing in our faith. We all live our lives in layers like the corn husk. When we peel each layer of ourselves away and share our faith walk, we help others grow as well. Like the tops of the corn all frazzled and brown, if we don't stay in motion with Jesus, we become lifeless.

Life is hard. God didn't promise that it would be easy, but we can grow mighty and strong during our growing seasons if we rely on Jesus to nourish our needs. Driving past these corn fields, it's obvious that the harvest this year will be abundant. Draw nearer to Jesus, lean in and trust. Our growing seasons have greater clarity when we rely on Him to get us through these great seasons of change in our lives.

So neither he who plants is anything nor he who waters, but [only] God Who makes it grow and become greater 1 Corinthians 3:7

CHANGING OF SEASONS

HAVE YOU SEEN the glory of Jesus in the changing of seasons? Everywhere you turn, you'll find a piece of Him. The turning leaves, dropping from the tree to the ground, are His love notes, gentle reminder that His grace is falling on you every minute of your day.

Today, seek His love and find Him in the corners of your heart. Look around, and you'll see a bit of Him tucked away. He's just waiting to offer you His love. As you breathe in the fall air, breathe in His essence, for Jesus is everywhere you are. Fall in love with Him all over again, and again, and again!

When we seek Jesus, we'll find Him. Search with all your heart!

Now set your mind and heart to seek (inquire of and require as your vital necessity) the Lord your God. Arise and build the sanctuary of the Lord God, so that the ark of the covenant of the Lord and the holy vessels of God may be brought into the house built to the Name and renown of the Lord. 1 Chronicles 22:19

THOUGHT FOR TODAY

Just love!

Love without judging.

Love as your own.

Love with laughter.

Love with a sympathetic ear.

Love and cherish your days, your life.

Love with an open heart.

Love beyond measure.

Love until your heart fills up.

Love the broken, the shattered, those hurting.

Love the breath God gave you.

Love His word. It's filled with love.

This is my commandment: that you love one another [just] as I have loved you John 15:12

23RD PSALM

THERE'S A PLACE where you can find sanctuary in the stillness and grace of God. Where a pool of crystal blue bathes the grassy shoreline, the beauty of a summer day unfolds right before your eyes. The water is calm and still. Your reflection flawless as you look upon yourself. Your beauty astounding as you see yourself in the glistening waters, exactly how God sees you.

Time stands still as the warm breezes embrace your total being and you know you're protected by God. You can feel His presence in the beauty of the day. Take delight in quenching your thirst in the cold, crystal waters that flow. The all-too-familiar calling to leave this oasis and reenter your chaotic world becomes harshly known. Take refuge in knowing along the way, that God will guide your path and lead you out of darkness.

As you hunger for more guidance and love from God the Almighty Father, you're revived right in front of your enemies. Your heart explodes with love and gratitude for your Father. You're reborn and reawakened to the love and light from above. His divine presence is so strong, you're able to break through the chains of your life bondage. Head home to a life of living joy, knowing that God's providing all you have and all you need.

Today is your breakthrough day, as God provides the vision that all you are is because of Him. He's preparing a place for you in heaven, at His right side. In His time you'll dwell with Him in the house of the Lord forever.

The Lord is my Shepherd [to feed, to guide and to shield me], I shall not lack. He makes me lie down in [fresh, tender] green pastures; He leads me beside the still and restful waters. He refreshes and restores my life myself); He leads me in the paths of righteousness [uprightness and right standing with Him – not for my earning it, but] for His name's sake. Yes, though I walk through the [deep, sunless] valley of the shadow of death, I will fear or dread no evil, for You are with me; Your rod [to protect] and Your staff [to guide], they comfort me. You prepare a table before me in the presence of my enemies. You anoint my head with oil; my [brimming] cup runs over. Surely or only goodness, mercy, and unfailing love shall follow me all the days of my life, and through the length of my days the house of the Lord [and His presence] shall be my dwelling place. Psalm 23

HIS GRACE

WE TAKE BACK our day, regroup, and get ready for God's golden opportunities. Armed with His grace and undeniable love. Pure joy pierces our heart, amps up our joy meter because He is the only one. No imitation or copycat, God's the real deal. You are His beloved.

Remember that your bloodline is filled with grace.

As you rise for the day, know that you're royalty – His princesses and princes. You're only a visitor here on this Earth. We are tied to Him. Shout it out: – "Thank You, Jesus, for your grace!" Selah.

Breathe Him in. You are His. You're a royal. Now act that way. Know that you're loved by a man who died to know you. Feel your heart amp up. That's grace. That's the joy of being loved even when we don't deserve it. He just loves, and that's the best story ever written.

And because you [really] are [His] sons, God has sent the [Holy] Spirit of His Son into our hearts, crying, Abba (Father)! Father! Galatians 4:6

GEMSTONES

LIFE IS LIKE a gemstone. A gemstone can't be polished without friction. Our lives are full of friction, trials that polish us into beautiful gems. When you allow Jesus into your heart, allow Him to work in your life, you'll shine more brilliantly. The stronger your faith becomes, the more love and joy you will feel and share. Be faithful to Jesus. He'll guide you through your trials to polish you into a shining gem. Be proud of who you are in Christ. He sees a gem every time.

Wrap your arms around your loved ones, look them in the eye, and tell them how much they're treasured. Realize you're God's treasured one, a diamond in the rough. Allow Him to polish you with undying love and grace until you shine. Look around, notice and give thanks for the blessings you'd miss if they went away tomorrow. Thank God for His divine intervention in your life. Find your joy in Him, knowing He's protecting you and that He loves you deeply. Shine like a diamond today!

For you are a holy people [set apart] to the Lord your God; and the Lord has chosen you to be a peculiar people to Himself, above all the nations on the earth. Deuteronomy 14:2

ONE THOUSAND PRAISES

ONE THOUSAND PRAISES wouldn't be enough to thank You for all you've done in our lives, Lord. As the hoot owl calls the evening's bliss and tucks the sun in for its evening rest, I praise You.

You are the keeper of our hearts and souls. We lift up our world to You as we slowly unwind from this day. On the other side of our world are those who are just waking up. May You beckon them to hear Your soft whispers of love. As their day breaks with a newness from the Son, may they fall to their knees and praise You.

Bless us in all we do. Let our hearts beat for You like 10,000 drums in unison. Hear our love for You resonate across the Earth.

Amen.

I will extol You, my God, O King; and I will bless Your name forever and ever [with grateful, affectionate praise]. Every day [with its new reasons] will I bless You [affectionately and gratefully praise You]; yes, I will praise Your name forever and ever. Psalm 145:1-2

DAYBREAK

THERE'S THIS CALM at the break of dawn when the moon exchanges places with the sun as it greets the new day. After the calm and a brief rustling of the wind, the earth acknowledges the sun rising into daylight. This exchange, this energy, can be felt in your soul as our world wakes up and comes alive.

The leaves rustle in rhythm to the gentle breeze, cheering on the sun rising in the east. Today, as our world wakes up, may you feel the Son of God flutter in your heart. He watches over us night and day, bringing a warmth and light into our hearts.

Lift up your hands and praise Him, for today you're renewed in Him.

Turn us to Yourself, O Lord, and we shall be turned and restored! Renew our days of old! Lamentations 5:21

ORBIT WITH THE SON

IT TAKES ONE year for our Earth to orbit the sun! How many trips have you taken around the sun, trusting in the Son?

Each year that the earth orbits the sun is a gift from God. How will you spend this year orbiting the Son?

Make the Son the center of your life, every minute of your day. Trust the Son. His love is timeless.

For the Lord your God is He Who goes with you to fight for you against your enemies to save you. Deuteronomy 20:4

LIFE IS A GIFT

LIFE IS A gift, a fragile gift that should be opened slowly. When time chases us into the future, we become caught up in trying to keep up. Sometimes we forget how truly precious life is. The here and now is important – how we spend our days, who we spend them with, and how we treat those we love.

When expectations run high, it's important to rely on Jesus to show us kindness and a loving heart. If we become caught up in how we think things should be, we'll never find joy or peace. If only for a moment, check and recheck yourself. How are you treating those around you? If you're not treating them with a Christ-like heart of love and compassion, then it's time to have a heart to heart with Jesus. Pray for His guidance, and ask Him to change your heart, so you may truly love those around you. Ask God to remove all the judgmental thoughts. After all, it's not about what we want for our life. It's about what God wants for us.

A new heart will I give you and a new spirit will I put within you, and I will take away the stony heart out of your flesh and give you a heart of flesh. And I will put my Spirit within you and cause you to walk in My statutes, and you shall heed My ordinances and do them. Ezekiel 36:26-27.

TEACH ME TO BREATHE

TEACH ME TO remain in the moment, Lord … to not get so exasperated by life's daily ups and downs … to be kind to my children when they are screaming and out of control. Teach me to realize they can have meltdowns, too. Teach me to let go of the routine. Remind me that life's a gift. Remind me to find joy in every little thing.

Teach me to have a kind heart and to be patient in all I do. Teach me to breathe. Teach me to rely on You for strength and to know You are in control of my circumstances. Lord, remind me that all I have to do is breathe.

Teach me to take a moment and share in conversations with You. Teach me to rely on You for everything, especially when life's daily struggles are ridiculously hard. Lord, teach me to breathe and to take in the day with joy because You are right beside me, guiding me all the way.

But those who wait for the Lord [who expect, look for, and hope in Him] shall change and renew their strength and power; they shall lift their wings and mount up [close to God] as eagles [mount up to the sun]; they shall run and not be weary, they shall walk and not faint or become tired. Isaiah 40:31

SPECK OF SAND (NOTES FROM GOD)

IF YOU WERE but a speck of sand in a desert, I'd find you from a million miles away for I knew where you'd be at this exact moment in time.

I adore and cherish you. You're my finest treasure, my child. I've longed to hear your voice call out my name. I find joy in you seeking and loving me. Know with me, you'll want for nothing. I will help you feel joy, and your heart will overflow with my love. I have loved you since before you were born and will love you until the end of time.

For God so greatly loved and dearly prized the world that He [even] gave up His only begotten (unique) Son, so that whoever believes in (trusts in, clings to, relies on) Him shall not perish (come to destruction, be lost) but have eternal (everlasting) life. John 3:16

JESUS IS

Jesus is your righteousness.

He's your redemption.

He's the reason you walk with grace.

Jesus is where you find rest.

Turn your eyes to Him.

In the light of His glory and grace, you will find peace.

There once stood a wall deep and wide, tall and strong.

But by His blood, He broke down this wall of sin, and by His mercy, Jesus died for all mankind.

For He is [Himself] our peace (our bond of unity and harmony). He has made us both [Jew and Gentile] one [body], and has broken down (destroyed, abolished) the hostile dividing wall between us. Ephesians 2:14

BLUEPRINTS OF LIFE (NOTES FROM GOD)

YOU'RE THE ILLUSTRATOR of your own story. You hold the key to your future, living your life through Me. Today is the day I made specifically for you.

Drink in the sunshine and feel the breezes of life.

Today, you are made new through Me. Trust in Me, and your blueprint of life will be changed forever.

No longer will you yearn for your past, as your present and future are far too exciting to look back on and yearn for.

I'll walk with you as your journey continues into greatness, the greatness I intended for your life. This life is for you to enjoy. Open the door and walk through. No one can take this adventure from you.

Come on! What are you waiting for? It's time to change the blueprint of your life, ask Me into your heart. It's time to receive your birthright, your gift of eternal life with Me in Heaven.

As you have therefore received Christ, [even] Jesus the Lord, [so] walk (regulate your lives and conduct yourselves) in union with and conformity to Him. Colossians 2:6

CLEAN SLATE

WHEN YOU ASK God for the forgiveness of your sins, you are granted "a clean slate."

From this day forward, you can move with grace knowing you are forgiven and God resides in your heart.

Allow His love to wash over you. Enter into your days refreshed and renewed.

Shine His light wherever you go.

Live your life Christ-centered.

Live your life for Him.

There it was – the true Light [was then] coming into the world [the genuine, perfect, steadfast Light] that illumines every person. John 1:9

POSSIBILITIES

Life is short
Live it
Love is rare
Grab it
Dreams are real
Chase them
Fear is a life stealer and a liar
God is with you.
Memories are sweet
Cherish your God-given life.

Jesus looked at them and said, With men this is impossible, but all things are possible with God. Matthew 19:26

A SURREAL LIFE

THIS LIFE, THIS crazy life is unimaginably beautiful. Look around you and gaze at the magnificent life God has given you. From the eyes of your beautiful children to the steadfast love of your spouse, family or friends; you are indeed blessed, and this life is real! Pinch yourself and believe.

Selah

All that is and all that is yet to come is from above!

Look up and thank Him for the blessings. Thank you, Lord, for this beautiful life.

For the rest, brethren, whatever is true, whatever is worthy of reverence and is honorable and seemly, whatever is just, whatever is pure, whatever is lovely and lovable, whatever is kind and winsome and gracious, if there is any virtue and excellence, if there is anything worthy of praise, think on and weigh and take account of these things [fix your minds on them]. Philippians 4:8

EVERY HAIR COUNTED

NOW, IF GOD keeps track and knows how many hairs are on your head - do not fear, for you are worth far more in God's eyes.

If God keeps track of every fiber of our being, there is nothing too small that you can't talk to Him about. Nothing!

God's love for you is infinitely immeasurable. He's totally and intensely involved in every minute of your day. So, when you talk to Him, pray to Him about every tiny detail of your life. He loves to hear from you.

The more you rely on Him instead of yourself, the more He hears. He is faithful and you have His full attention, every minute of the day He waits for you to call on Him. So cast every care to Him.

But even the very hairs of your head are all numbered. Fear not, then you are of more value than many sparrows. Therefore everyone who acknowledges Me before men and confesses Me [out of state of oneness with Me], I will also acknowledge him before My Father Who is in heaven and confess [that I am abiding in] him. Matthew 10:30-32

DON'T GIVE UP

WE DON'T GIVE up loving because Jesus is love. We don't give in to giving up, we get up and show up because Jesus showed up for us. On the day He cooed His way into our lives wrapped in swaddling clothes, He was born to save the world. He knows our every heartbeat. He knows when our mind is weary from talk of our country turning sour. He knows when we need to just rest in Him. After a blissful, peaceful moment spent with Him, we will have a revival of sorts as we get back up; because it's the only place we belong – not in the gray or dark place but in the light with Him.

And just when our heart's sinking and our bodies are just plain worn, He will come and shine His light so bright, because we were born of Him. We're heirs to the throne and nothing that others say can take that away.

Slay the words that bring fear to our minds, dice the thoughts that we know are the polar opposite of what He tells us in His Word.

Remember His promise of more to come, look for the doors, the door to calm, the door to knowledge, the door to peace, the door to Him and walk through because we're His people and His people are brave. He gives us strength to keep going.

He is our brave, He is our peace, our Prince of peace.

All the words of my mouth are righteous (upright and in right standing with God); there is nothing contrary to the truth or crooked in them. They are all plain to him who understands [and opens his heart], and right to those who find knowledge [and live by it]. Proverbs 8:8-9

START A REVOLUTION!

WHEN YOU GROW weary from a day that's chock full of draining tasks, whether it be your job, errands, dealing with tired children, or any of your everyday appointments, stick your arm out your car window and lift it up to Jesus. While you're driving off to one of life's great adventures; roll down your window, turn up your radio, and sing out loud.

Raise your hand up to Jesus. Yes! Stick your arm out the window, and raise it up. Praise Jesus for all your days. Drink Him in. Become Sondrenched, and receive your energizing gift of Jesus' love! What a joy for Him to look down and see His children reaching up for His love. He will smile on us all.

Be bold for Jesus and watch your day change.

Amen.

Lift up your hands in holiness and to the sanctuary and bless the Lord [affectionately and gratefully praise Him]! Psalm 134:2

CHAOTIC WORLD

LORD, HOW I love Thee. I look to the sky and feel your presence all around me.

The clouds whisk on by in beautiful formations, made gracefully by You.

I hear your voice in the bird that sings, his melody so sweet, so true. I hear You say, "I love you," and I know. I feel your strength rise up in me. Long is this day, in a chaotic world where people don't know You. Those with their sharp tongues and uncaring ways have left me tired and worn. I long for your presence to remain in me all day. I call out to You, but I'm derailed by the cries of the people around me, and I'm thrown off track.

I need You in constant motion in my life, a continuous reminder that your love and strength will never cease. I will remain true to You. Help me to not be thrown off track, by the battle of mundane things I face daily. Remain in me, help me stay focused. Keep me on track Lord so I can walk with grace, and love those around me. Keep me in your ever-loving presence, How I love Thee. Help me to notice every tiny moment, every cloud, star, sun and moon, for these are my constant reminders of your love.

Then I [Wisdom] was beside Him as a master and director of the work; and I was daily His delight, rejoicing before Him always, Rejoicing in His inhabited Earth and delighting in the sons of men. Proverbs 8:30-31

WHO IS OUR JESUS?

HAVE YOU EVER had someone in your life that meant more to you than the moon and stars? This is a different kind of love, stronger than the love of your spouse or child. It's that feeling you had when you saw your baby for the very first time, perfection, and beauty beyond comprehension. This is when you see Jesus.

Jesus is everywhere, in the flowers, the trees, in the wind and rain. He's in the faces of your family and friends, but the most significant thing is when Jesus takes residency in you. That's when your heart and soul change. Your heart changes and your mind evolves, and you see a brilliance in everything around you. You notice enchanted evenings and see stars, not as stars, but as the many people you want to touch. The people that you hope will come know Jesus like you. You become bolder in your faith and challenge yourself to not skip a beat, to not miss a moment. You appreciate every breath, every intricate, tiny, minuscule particle on the planet because everything's God breathed. Everything here on earth is a part of Jesus and comes from Him. You crave more of Him.

Everything in life is more vibrant, and joy becomes second nature. Jesus loves you, lives in you and He blankets you with protection. You are His.

Who is your Jesus?

UNDO US LORD

HE WHO MADE us can undo us. In this world where everything seems to be out of control, and it feels as if all of your people are lost, broken and beaten down -undo us. Take us back to your glory, our glory in You!

Help us to spread love – to love our neighbor no matter what color – no matter what religion – no matter what.

Take us back Lord, to only knowing You, only wanting You, only wanting to live like You.

Stop the hate in our world. "Satan take a back seat" – Our Heavenly Father is our God, our Lord of Lords. He's set the tone for our day.

Undo us, Lord. Take us back to only needing You!

We get on bended knee and pray – Pray for the mending, the renewing of our world, your world. Undo us, Lord, for we only want You.

And I will give them a new heart to know (recognize, understand, and be acquainted with) Me, that I am the Lord; and they will be My people, and I will be their God, for they will return to Me with their whole heart. Jeremiah 24:7

HEY, YOU! (LOVE NOTES FROM GOD)

HEY, YOU! YES, you sitting there with your hand on your head, wondering how you'll ever finish out this week. Mind racing, heart beating, and life just got real. Yes, you, the strong one, the bold one who thinks tomorrow will definitely be worse than today.

Feel my whisper in the moment, "I AM, I am the one who breathed life into you and feels every teardrop, every heartache, and every pain. I feel your joy, your smiles, and your radiant face beam when you've exhausted yourself to the max. When you've done everything you could, breathe in the day and exhale knowing I AM. I am with you on a dark dreary night, when your soul is crying out to me. I am the fire that burns so bright inside of you, and if you'd only leap to the next level of what I have in store for you, you'd know.

"You'd know I AM. I am the one who's there when you cry out in anguish, 'Why don't you save the world?' I AM the last love in your heart that you must release to those around you. I AM the one who can soften your heart. I AM the smile on your loved ones face, the hug of a friend, your everlasting love. I AM. Here on all the days, you are longing for something more. I AM."

DO YOU NOT KNOW?

Have you not known? Have you not heard? The everlasting God, the Lord, the creator of the ends of Earth, does not faint or grow weary; there is no searching of His understanding. He gives power to the faint and weary, and to Him who has no might He increases strength [causing it to multiply and making it abound] Isaiah 40:28-29

DO NOT GIVE UP - even when the week seems to drag on.

You number and record my wanderings; put my tears into Your bottle - are they not in your book? Then shall my enemies cry out; this I know, for God is for me. In God have I put my trust and confident reliance; I will not be afraid. What can man do to me? Psalm 56:8-11

HE'S NOT DONE – Praise Him non-stop for he'll bring you great joy, and He will hold you by night, and he'll lift you up during the day – you are never alone. His healing power shall and will be upon you. When you grow weary, draw nearer and never let Him go, for He has you. You are His finest treasure, and this race called life shall be won! Your prize is your citizenship in Heaven.

PRAYER DURING HARD TIMES

LORD, BLESS US during this season of life. You know, the season of change and enduring more than we ever thought we could? How we love You, raise our arms up to You. It's You who is always there by our side. How magnificently stunning is your grace! We are in awe of your loving heartstrings entwined in ours. You breathe into our lives the love of our eternal bliss. We're humbled at your feet!

Nothing can stop our heart beats for your love. Fill us up with compassion and kindness. Allow us to show others how it's You that can fill their hearts to capacity with Your love. Let them see You in us. Let them crave You through us. May we drink You in, and quench our thirst to the core of our soul, so we too may feel the green pastures of life! Amen.

The Lord is my Strength and my Song, and He has become my Salvation; this is my God, and I will praise Him, my father's God, and I will exalt Him. Exodus 15:2

FINEST BLESSING

MAY TODAY BE your finest blessing and may the dramas in your life be seen only on your favorite movies or TV. May God bless your life with joy and laughter so you may literally "dance and sing in the rain."

May you find peace in your inner soul. May you resolve to realize that all you have and all you are, is a gift to be thankful for daily.

Set your standards high today, higher than ever before. Adore your life. Waste not a moment grumbling or being sad. Today is your gift, open it and be thankful!

Today, open the door to your life with wonder. This life, this day is specifically made for you ... Embrace it and shine!

May blessings (praise, laudation, and eulogy) be to the God and Father of our Lord Jesus Christ (the Messiah) who has blessed us in Christ with every spiritual (given by the Holy Spirit) blessing in the heavenly realm! Ephesians 1:3

G-R-A-C-E

SHE SAT THERE with a bag, and with a sigh of relief she dumped it out. She shook it a few times until all the mistakes, the self-contempt and the multitude of problems she was carrying piled up on the table. She looked across the table at Him, and all she could see was the glow circling around his head. Her Sweet Redeemer had come, and she finally dumped all the issues of the day, weeks, even months onto the table just like He had asked. She sat there hands on her head, and when she looked up with tears streaming down her face, the pile in front of her was gone! The pile that was once in front of her had been replaced with golden letters shining bright, glistening in His glow. When she looked at the letters laid out in front of her she saw G-R-A-C-E. She looked over at Him and he said, "I am making you brand new! I am giving you a clean slate. Let's start this week together." She looked Him straight in the eye and sweetly whispered, "Amen."

Roll your works upon the Lord [commit and trust them wholly to Him; He will cause your thoughts to become agreeable to His will, and] so shall your plans be established and succeed. Proverbs 16:3

BREATHE

LORD, WE BREATHE You in, and on the exhale, we realize all these beautiful breaths are Your "love notes" to our bodies! How intricately You designed us to be.

On these days our struggle can be so real – so hard, and we know You wait for us to call on you. You trump struggles, fear and the multitude of problems that blanket our days. Sometimes, unknowingly we retreat to silence because our ultra-sensitive hearts need to be rejuvenated by You. Even in the silence Lord, when we're tired and weep from exhaustion, You are here. You beckon us to come closer, to breathe in your essence. Sometimes it's just hard Lord when the joy-filled moments dissolve into the unknown, overtaken by feelings of just needing to be in silence.

Bring us back to the top Lord, to the top of our game, so we can once again push away the lies in our heads. Allow our bodies to breathe and feel your love notes on the exhale. Fill us back up, grant us rest and peace. Thank You for Your gift, your presence in our lives, Your promise of the Lamb – Your Son, Jesus Christ. Help us to become Sondrenched and find joy again.

In Your Son Jesus' sweet name,

Amen.

LOVE NOTES FROM GOD

JUST BREATHE, AND let me be. As the waves rush to shore, I am in you. As the sun sets in the west, it is me.

I know you're dealing. I know you're trying. I know you are seeing a tiny bit of me through the storms. Just breathe, just breathe and let me be with you.

I'm there with you crying when you think you're dying. It is me you feel in these moments. I feel you trying to find me, and I will let you, oh, I will let you find comfort in me.

So, when the rain is falling, and you think that it's calling you to a place you need to be, will you please allow me to dry your tears knowing, that the place you need to be is with me.

Let me be with you, it's the only place you'll find me, I'm always with you, it's the only place I want to be.

So everyone who hears these words of Mine and acts upon them [obeying them] will be like a sensible (prudent, practical, wise) man who built his house upon the rock. Matthew 7:24

LEAP OF FAITH

MAY GOD AWAKEN you today to all you possess in Him. May He open your eyes to the reality that you are His! May you refuse to let your disappointments define you, instead may you stand in that one place where you hesitate to take a leap of faith and jump! See His vision, and envision your life remade and may you experience a revival of faith in that very place. Instead of rehashing your losses, be determined to remember His promises, they're truer than your circumstances.

Today's a good day to embrace your faith, to give thanks and to worship the One who keeps His promises. Jesus loves you and He is faithful to His word.

May His love define you and His promises establish in your heart the wisdom to know who you truly are - uniquely made and loved by Him. You've got everything you need in Him. Have a blessed day.

For everything God has created is good, and nothing is to be thrown away or refused if it is received with thanksgiving. For it is hallowed and consecrated by the word of God and by prayer. 1 Timothy 4:4-5

MADE FOR YOU

BREATHE IN THE smell of the summer day and know, know this day was made specifically for you. Inhale God's beauty and explore and place this day in your memory bank, a special deposit known only to you. Cherish these days.

Implore the Lord of your life to keep them coming because you adore these days. Refuel your soul in all of God's wonders.

Each day becomes more significant in its own way because each day we age a little more. Listen to the bird song that beckons your attention, know God is speaking. Through the cricket song and gentle breeze whispering on by, God speaks "I love you." As you listen, send up praises, for these sweet days are made especially for you.

Selah.

He has made everything beautiful in its time. He also has planted eternity in men's hearts and minds [a divinely implanted sense of purpose working through the ages which nothing under the sun but God alone can satisfy], yet so that men cannot find out what God has done from beginning to end. Ecclesiastes 3:11

MONDAYS

IT'S THAT CRAZY fun day, the day everyone dreads -- Monday! The alarm goes off, and you roll over wishing the clock would magically slow down to three hundred tick tocks per second! Your wandering angel comes into your room in his superman jammies and you know, these moments are golden! Superman flies across the bed like never before, and for the first time of many you announce, "I am in love with a superhero!" His little toes cold against your body are a welcome response to this first Monday, your superhero's new day. Because you know you've done everything your God-driven soul has whispered, he is the magical boy of your dreams.

Savor this day, this beautiful day where God gave you the superhero of your dreams. Because you know this boy, this little boy is everything and more, savor this day all the more. Lock it down in your memory bank and leave it there for another day when your superhero is testing your strength. Remember, his strong will is a gift from God because your little superhero is at times more determined than the ant dragging a morsel of food back to his home. This little boy, this God gift from heaven, is fabulously becoming the man of your dreams!

Behold, children are a heritage from the Lord, the fruit of a womb a reward. Psalm 127:3

LOVE

THIS LIFE COMES with no instruction manual, no book of joy, hope or love. All these things come neatly packed in our hearts, just waiting for us to find them. Our children, our family, and friends can sometimes leave us so drained, yet so loved. So why does it have to feel so heart wrenchingly hard when they fall?

Love – the unexplainable, fill up your soul feeling that no one should ever be without.

Love – the love of a parent, child or friend is just this, ultimately the divine, our Jesus drenching us with the purest feeling on the planet.

God's love

So, when you become overburdened, exhausted to the core, remember, God is shining His light on you and He will never leave nor forsake you. Find your joy, hope, and love in Him.

I have loved you, [just] as the Father has loved me; abide in My love [continue in His love with Me]. John 15:9

FAITH FOLLOWERS

WE LIVE, WE laugh, we cry. We are sometimes boastful and too wrapped up in life to care. Then, we take a moment and place a memory, a mind movie from our memory bank on days when life is hard. We withdraw it and play it for hours. It's when we play this memory in our mind, we realize we have it all! The family that loves us, children that adore us, and our friends that take our breath away. It's a life given to us by our Almighty Father. It's your life and how you live it, and it's about who you are in Christ. It's how we live our life, how we set the pace for those watching, that determines how we walk as a Faith Follower.

Your life on this planet is set to the beat of God Moments, little blessings, huge happenings and tiny falls to our earth that comprise our day. How we rise, how we treat each moment is how we are defined in Christ. How we influence others with our attitudes, good or bad is up to us. Free Will. Give it all you've got. Our days are precious, we only get one shot at this life, make it count for Jesus. Be the life changer – be that someone to someone else.

Be the "mind movie" that someone will play later. Be the memory for someone to remember later and smile. Be the one that is an important part of their life. Show them you care. Be the memory that Jesus would want us to be. Be the love of life, the keeper of hearts, and make someone's life memorable, because you are God's greatest treasure.

CLEAR OUR VISION

LORD–WE PRAY FOR the broken-hearted today. The lost souls who need You in their lives. We ask for strength for those seeking to break free from the things that hold their hearts hostage. May they have a longing in their hearts for You. May You stir in them compassion for themselves and the world. Make the longing in their hearts so strong, that they become like Daniel facing the Goliaths in their lives. May they fight for their own hearts, the hearts loved by You. Show them the warrior way to rise up stronger than before. Allow them to see that You are at the front of the ship driving them to a joyful, inspired Jesus filled life. Let the light in us shine so bright, it binds those who don't see and help their vision to become clearer than ever before. Let them see their life made whole again by You.

As long as we reach out to You Lord, You are the only light that shines bright, never dulls our senses. Take our hands Lord and guide us to Eden, where heartache doesn't exist because we regain strength in You. Guard these beautiful souls and show them their beautiful God made faces, in the reflection of the crystal blue waters. May they find peace in knowing that being loved by You is all they need, and that their heart beats for You. Amen.

GOOD MORNING!

TAKE HEART IN knowing, you are loved. Now, this love's far greater than anything you've ever known. This love is God's love drenching you in His pure mercy and grace.

This love is unconditional, no strings attached. Oh, how He loves you, died for you and allows you to live as a forgiven soul filled with grace.

Look up, raise your hands up and receive it all.

Receive His greatest gift; open it, tear it open and let it fill you up! God's love is your gift, all day every day. He never leaves you.

Selah.

He must increase, but I must decrease. [He must grow more prominent; I must grow less so.] John 3:30

SPEAK IN THE SILENCE

HOW OFTEN DO you try to sit in silence? How often do you sit outside in the early morning mist and just listen? Silence, broken by a car hurrying by or birds singing. There is this bird, this one bird that sings relentlessly in the trees, what if it was us? What if we're so relentless in speaking of our faith we never stop? Would there be silence? Would people stop in their tracks to listen? Do you share Jesus, or do you listen? Do you wait for someone to speak of Him, and yet you remain silent? If we don't speak of Him how will others hear?

Let not the world be silent, but let the words of Jesus flow from our lips like the songbird in the tree. Be relentless in your faith, so we may become like a flock of birds singing in unison for Jesus.

So faith comes by hearing [what is told], and what is heard comes by the preaching [of the message that came from the lips] of Christ the Messiah Himself. Romans 10:17

MAKE IT AN EXTRAORDINARY DAY

WAKE UP TODAY and be thankful. You woke up because of God's plan for your life. Is it an ordinary or extraordinary day?

Choices … plans … the determination to just get through another day, or are you going to make someone's day?

We are chosen by Him to be His disciples – for those in the streets, those in the office, those in the grocery store or gas station, those at daycare or the doctor's office, even those you meet on vacation. How you respond to others, impacts your day as well as theirs.

Who shall you be today? Fun-loving, joy-filled or full of remorse and troubles?

Everyone you meet is a learning link in your faith walk. Will you open your heart or close it off? There's so many that need grace today. There's so many that need a touch of the Son. They need to see His love shine through you. Those in need or those that need to teach you something.

Life lessons, learn as you go – God wants to show you the way.

Oh God, You have taught me from my youth, and hitherto have I declared Your wondrous works. Psalm 71:17

SEE HIS GREATNESS

LORD, YOUR MERCY is like a giant river flowing peacefully through a rocky hillside. No matter how rough our lives become, You always grant mercy that is so beautiful, it can make a heart melt, often take our breath away.

Leave us breathless today. Help us show others this great mercy that You bestow upon us.

As your love flows through us, may we express this love to others. May we express this love by shining your beautiful light. May our love for you flow through us like a gentle stream flowing through a lush hillside. May we help your sheep find You in the greenest of pastures.

Amen

You have granted me life and favor, and Your providence has preserved my spirit. Job 10:12

BEAUTIFUL HEART

I WATCHED THE man at the red light shaking his fist, as he waited for the light to change. Who is he? What's his story? What made him so angry, so in a hurry? Are you the same as yesterday? Do you still carry around anger, fear, grief or pain? I wish for you, I wish you could see the man in the moon, the face of the Son waiting for you, longing for you. He has your ticket! Your ticket to freedom, and a new you for today!

He's gentle, kind, loving and He waits. He waits for your beauty to shine through, your smile, your laughter, and your joy. His heart aches with yours. He is that connected to you! He made you, but He waits. Who are you in Him? Are you the same as yesterday? What do others see? Do they know? Do they see? Do they see a beautiful soul? God sees, and He's holding your beautiful heart waiting on you.

Lord, to You we pray for our hearts to beat in tune with yours. Unleash our hurt, pain, and fear, help us to heal.

The Egyptians had a beautiful belief about death. When their souls were at the entrance to heaven, the guards asked two question before they entered: Have you found joy in your life? Has your life brought joy to others?

Your presence has brought joy to so many. Who are you today, bound to your pain, or bound to God's blessings and joy?

WHY NOT?

YOU KNOW ALL the months, those hard months of waiting on God? Months you've spent asking, "Why?" Asking yourself over and over, "Why me?" Stomping your feet and not understanding, yet going through the motions of life.

Well, "Why not?" Why not take the time to just be, be in tune with God? Don't ask any questions, just be. When you once again hear yourself asking why, don't talk about it to anyone, just lay down with Jesus and just be. Listen for His whisper, His gentle touch, but look for His beauty too. When you can't go on, and your bone tired, when the answers aren't coming, as frustrating as it may be – Trust! Because whenever in your life has He ever done you wrong? Whenever in your life has Jesus not been by your side? So, to be or not to be, it's up to you. People will tell you what to do. Oh, they will have their own opinions, but then, when is it God's opinion? So, the next time you ask why, when your world is spinning and answers aren't coming, just ask Jesus, and put out your hand to Him. When you feel Him grab your heartstrings, this is when you'll know, you'll know the nearer you draw to Him, the nearer you are to prayers answered. So, just be and trust Him.

You will show me the path of life; in Your presence is fullness and joy, at Your right hand there are pleasures forevermore. Psalm 16:11

ENTWINED WITH GOD

LORD, AS WE "take heart," may our hearts entwine with yours. May we have the heart to see those who struggle, the sick, the single moms and dads with hearts weeping when they're so tired, those fighting addiction and those with broken hearts. Tie our hearts together. Loop our hearts around those who need the refuel of their heart, as it empties from a hard day. Teach us, Lord, to be the deal breakers, the heart healers who lead those string of hearts to You. May we walk in tune to your heartbeats and lift them to You. Teach us to have hearts of gold that bust at the seams with your love, gushing out onto those who need it most. Show us and guide us to those who need to hear your heart song. May our hearts beat in tune to You. May we breathe in your grace and exhale your love just as You once did when you took on human skin and walked amongst the broken here on earth. Teach us to walk in unison with You. Guide us to be your prayer warriors.

Lord - Hope is in our hearts – may we be beating hearts for You. May we show empathy to the broken hearts and shine your love on those in need. May we be a generation of hearts entwined with You. Amen.

And this is the confidence (the assurance, the privilege of boldness) which we have in Him: [we are sure] that if we ask anything (make any request) according to His will (in agreement with His own plan), He listens to and hears us. 1 John 5:14

SAVOR EACH MOMENT

THE ALLURE OF God is like the enticing scent of pine on Christmas morning. Butterflies and candy canes, and the finest hour waiting on the Christ child can be yours 365 days a year! God's calling you, pulling you back into check, after a whirlwind day of getting the kids off to school. He's longing for your attention, like the attention to detail we place on our child's school outfits and sports gear. We spend so much time getting the kids off to school, we forget about the small boy on the other side of our world who has to walk three miles to school in bare feet. We forget about this small boy who doesn't have a mom to help him pick out clothes. He doesn't have new clothes at all. He's lucky to have the tiny hut he lives in, as his mother died of HIV less than a month ago.

Don't take anything for granted, as your small child gets off the bus grumbling about the inadequate playground at school. Share with your child all things you are thankful for. Tell your child you are thankful for him or her. Take time to thank God for our beautiful children, and for others children as we pray for all of God's children all over the world. God spends so much time blessing us, if we don't take the time to be thankful, we will never be humbled, we'll never have enough. We'll never see and realize, God is all we need.

Take time today to savor the details, the beauty of God's world. One thing is clear, clear as the sky is blue … For God so loved this world, He gave His only true Son, for you and me. If we simply believe in this beautiful Christ Child, our Jesus, we shall not perish, but eternally we are all saved by His grace and everlasting love. We can experience the Christ child 365 days a year.

I give thanks to my God for you always when I mention you in my prayers, because I continue to hear of your love and of your loyal faith which you have toward the Lord Jesus and [which you show] toward all the saints God's consecrated people) [And I pray] that the participation in and sharing of your faith may produce and promote full recognition and appreciation and understanding and precise knowledge of every good [thing] that is ours in [our identification with] Christ Jesus [and unto His glory]. Philemon 1:4-6

PARACHUTE OF LOVE

HE WILL NOT forsake you, nor will He let you fall! His plan for your life, mmm absolutely stunning! Don't be afraid, He's got you, and you can free fall and leap in faith, for His parachute of love will open and save you.

Because who knew? He knew you were His chosen one, marked with His blood. All you have to do is follow His lead. When He speaks listen because He already knows. Because you are loved and what else do you need?

When you grow weary, unsure of where your life is headed, you can be reassured that God's plan is miraculous. Allow Him to plan your day, follow His lead.

I am convinced and sure of this very thing, that He Who began a good work in you will continue until the day of Jesus Christ [right up to the time of His return], developing [that good work] and perfecting and bringing it to full completion in you. Philippians 1:6

RIPPLE EFFECT

I WATCHED THESE massive raindrops fall, and as they did, the splashdown was magnificent! As each drop hit the surface of the ground, you could see it splash and watch the drop ripple out to the water's edge, touching everything around it in a circular motion.

I must tell you this - you have so much potential. You have the potential to bless others with your beautiful ways. You have so much to offer others. The lives you reach out to and touch today will start a ripple effect in another person's life. This ripple effect will lead others to touch another person's life, because of you! You can leave magnificent ripples on this earth, just by who God made you to be. Every kind word leads to another. How big will your circular span, your ripple effect of kindness grow?

Make a splash today! Be your beautiful self and watch the ripples take place. Jesus loves when you show and spread His joy! Send out ripples, share your magnificent self and how His love saved you.

UNLEASH A BEAUTIFUL WORLD

TODAY, LOOK FOR the possibilities God is placing in your life. Choose His favor and blessings, instead of trying to run life on your own. This great race called life can be more beautiful than we could ever imagine if we allow God to show us the possibilities. Giving up control for our life and trusting in Him, and praying about everything will unleash a beautiful world, more beautiful than we can imagine.

God in all His goodness continues to show us that if we just quit trying so hard to control it all, He can take us places we've never even dared to imagine. I want to see the possibilities today – how about you?

[Most] blessed is the man who believes in, trusts in, and relies on the Lord, and whose hope and confidence the Lord is. For he shall be like a tree planted by the waters that spreads out its roots by the river; and it shall not see and fear when heat comes; but its leaf shall be green. It shall not be anxious and full of care in the year of drought, nor shall it cease yielding fruit. Jeremiah 17:7-8

IT'S REALLY THAT SIMPLE

I WAKE UP today and I'm thankful. I pray a special blessing on your day. I pray that you'll delight in knowing how much God loves you. I remind you because I hope you know you're special to God. I pray safe travels for you, to and from work. I pray you will touch lives today like you've touched so many already. God is amazing, and He just plain loves, no added blah, blah, blah. It's just that simple.

Soak it up for a minute, it's a beautiful day, and you are a beautiful soul. Have a great day!

We need to express to others how much they've impacted our lives. We need to let others know how much we care for them. They need to know they're loved. You never know, we might be in Heaven tomorrow! God is coming for us, we don't know when, but all we need to radiate His love, it's really that simple.

If then you have been raised with Christ [to a new life, thus sharing His resurrection from the dead], aim at and seek the [rich eternal treasures] that are above, where Christ is seated at the right hand of God. And set your minds and keep them set on what is above (the higher things) not on the things that are on Earth. Colossians 3:1-2

RETHINK THE DAY

WHY DO SO many people dread the morning? It's a brand new day. It's a new day of possibilities. Why do so many dread the beginning of the week, Mondays in particular? Mondays are brand new, so are Tuesdays, Wednesdays, Thursdays, Fridays and Saturdays too! Christ makes us brand new all over again, each and every day – nothing but pure grace.

Rethink Mondays and all days. Life shouldn't be so hard, it should be a day of being renewed in Christ – seven days a week, every day of our life!

The angels are singing sweet melodies, sweet music to our ears. It's a beautiful day in Jesus. Rethink the Day and watch how easy it is to wake up every morning renewed in Him!

And be constantly renewed in the spirit of your mind [having a fresh mental and spiritual attitude]. And put on a new nature (the regenerate self) created in God's image, [Godlike] in true righteousness and holiness. Ephesians 4:23-24

WAVES OF FAITH

HAVE YOU EVER gone to the beach and seen beautiful sandcastles along the shoreline? Each one so unique in its own way. Some sandcastles remain longer than others, as the tide comes in and the waves wash over them whisking them away.

As we grow in our faith, we are built up like unique sandcastles. God's love pours into us like specks of sand, one speck of love after another, until we appear like a magnificent sandcastle, beautiful and unique in our own way. He transforms and renews our souls. When we remain faithful and stand tall, we grow like a sandcastle from the ground up beautiful in His likeness.

May you remain in Him. May your faith grow, may you find peace in Him, along the shoreline in life. May you remain unique and magnificent while embracing your day in the Son.

And now [brethren], I commit you to God [I deposit you to His charge, entrusting you to His protection and care]. And I commend you to the Word of His Grace [to the commands and counsels and promises of His unmerited favor]. It is able to build you up, and to give you [your rightful] inheritance among all God's set-apart ones (those consecrated, purified, and transformed of soul). Acts 20:32

CHAMPION OF GOD

WE'RE ALMOST TO the end of the week. The high hurdle in the middle of the week has been surpassed by the greatest of runners – you! Now let's make it one short stride to the end! Hand off the baton of grace to everyone who passes you by whether they have done you right or wrong! That is grace. It's time to set the pace to run to the end.

Breaths come in quick gulps, and as you swallow down that oxygen, breathe in grace and exhale those who have done you wrong! This week was made for champions, and you are a champion of God's grace. He's molding you into a winner to run against the enemy. Know you're a winner because God is right there running with you.

It's time to throw down those thoughts of discontent and become content with Jesus, for He's the golden trophy, the reason we race daily, for we race to His arms to ultimately slow down our day and find peace.

In You, O Lord, do I put my trust and seek refuge, let me never be put to shame or [have my hope in You] disappointed; deliver me in Your righteousness! Psalm 31:1

FOR YOU

HE STOOD THERE holding a sign, it simply read, "For you." As He turned to walk away, He bent down and picked up his bag. He didn't ask for anything, only for us to hold Him in our hearts. On He went, and with each step and each person He passed his baggage grew heavier until He reached his journey's end. It seemed as if He removed the turmoil from each person as he passed them by. We found out later that day He had died. He died for all of us, and we became consumed with grief.

The day after His death we longed for Him, missed His presence so. We found the bag He left at the top of the hill, it was empty. The bag was empty, but the imprints on the inside of the bag read SORROW, SINS, GRIEF, SUFFERING, PAIN and the list went on and on. He had taken all our burdens with him. He left nothing behind!

The next day He rose from the dead and replaced everyone's heavy burdens with a joy that no words could explain. Everyone knew and believed in Him. They knew they would see Him again. He invited all of them to His house, His paradise in Heaven! No longer would they have to suffer, for through Him, they were saved, all of us are saved!

DID YOU FEEL IT?

DID YOU FEEL it today? Did you feel the embrace this morning as your Heavenly Father wrapped you in His blanket of protection?

Wow! You are so loved, so adored, so undeniably His!

By the blood He shed, He claimed you.

He desperately wants you to know, He loves you and He is with you.

Don't forget your "blankie" as you head out today, He's got you!

But I will settle him (Him) in My house and in My kingdom forever; and his (His) throne shall be established forevermore. 1 Chronicles 17:14

IF ONLY

WHAT IF YOU did everything right? What if you are kind, generous with your love, money, and possessions? What if you noticed everything, everyone? What if you always smile and open doors for others? What if you help those in need, and you always say "thank you" and "hello," even if others do not? What if you get to work and never complain, take exactly the time you are allowed for breaks and lunch? What if you are the upbeat person who makes everyone's day? What if you were happy to just be in the moment, nonjudgmental basking in the glow of the day? What if we were like this all the time? Would we walk the Earth and change the world, or would the world be a better place that no longer needed change? If only the world could be this beautiful place. A place with no time constraints, no pain, no sickness, no hate. This could be Heaven! Get your God on and find it! Be Heaven on Earth, be Christ-like! Walk the Earth for Jesus, open the door and let Him into your heart, and watch those around you see Him in you.

But without faith it is impossible to please and be satisfactory to Him. For whoever would come near to God must [necessarily] believe that God exists and that He is the rewarder of those who earnestly and diligently seek Him [out]. Hebrews 11:6

I WANT TO FOLLOW YOU

OH, MY FATHER, You lead and I follow. There is nothing else on this tiny planet I want. I want nothing more than to be at peace and find solitude in my surroundings. I leave it all up to You, Lord. Your want, your will in my life, until we meet in Heaven. You feed me on your daily word.

As I search for your Godliness in my surroundings, your shining light helps me find truth. As You love me, Lord, teach me to love others. Forgive me for all my wrongdoings. I lift up those in my life who have hurt me. I ask for your loving mercy on those who have crossed my path unjustly. I am asking for your love, to fill my heart and theirs.

I no longer wish to do the things that take me off the God-driven path. Keep the doors closed that I shouldn't enter. Allow me to only enter those doors that will bring me joy. Allow me to show others the way to You.

For this is your world, your loving planet, and I want to share your love with those around me. Your will be done Lord until we meet here on Earth or in Heaven.

Let love for your fellow believers continue and be a fixed practice with you [never let it fail]. Hebrews 13:1,

GOD CELEBRATES YOU

TODAY GOD CELEBRATES you as you inhale upon awakening, and on the exhale ask yourself, when was the last time you celebrated you?

Today, celebrate your beauty, your job – good or bad, your health, your ability to make others smile, celebrate your joy in Christ.

God made you in His likeness – that's reason enough to celebrate. Find your joy today because you don't walk alone – Jesus is right there beside you.

Inhale and exhale this beautiful day -celebrate your life!

You will show me the path of life; in Your presence is fullness of joy, at Your right hand there are pleasures forevermore. Psalm 16:11

MOVING DAY

PRAY THIS PRAYER today, and watch things move in your life, and in the lives around you.

Lord, I want to see You move!

I believe and trust You to move in me, and change my life and the lives of those around me. Place those in my path that are seeking a touch of the Son. Use me to show kindness and wisdom and help those who are seeking You to find You, Lord. Place on my lips the words You want others to hear. Move in me, Lord. I want to see those around me who are hurting, find peace. Lord, move in those with addiction and change their addictions for only You. I'm asking You to move through us, and all of those who are reading this today! Lord, move in us, through us and use us for your glory! It's moving day Lord, move us in the right directions and open doors where we should walk. Slam those doors where we should not go. Move us to spread your joy and smile like your Son. Move us, Lord, and show us our life paths where we may do our best for You. We live and breathe for You, Lord. As sure as the sun shines, move us in ways You designed us to move.

Amen.

NEVER ALONE

AND HE STARTED packing. He placed everything in her bags - heartache, pain sickness, loneliness, fear, inadequacy, shame, and suffering. He pushed hard, stuffing it all into the bag. He stood there waiting, and as He did He took out a box that held His heart and gave it to her. He unraveled a blanket that read, "Protection," and He placed it around her. As she stood there not moving, He told her "I'll carry those heavy burdens. I love you, and this bag, well, you won't need it anymore. You no longer have to drag it around, I'm setting you free." He took her hand and they walked down the road.

You are never alone!

Call on Jesus. Pack your bags and start living the life He died for you to have, your life in Christ! Once He packs your bags, it comes with a no return policy, do not try to pick it back up. He already picked you, what are you waiting for?

It is the Lord Who goes before you; He will [march] with you; He will not fail you or let you go or forsake you; [let there be no cowardice or flinching, but] fear not, neither become broken [in spirit – depressed, dismayed, and unnerved with alarm]. Deuteronomy 31:8

THOUGHTS FOR TODAY

1. If you're always late, pray for God to help you to think ahead.
2. If you wish you could go back in time, you'll still have to do it all again. It's part of God's plan.
3. You were loved long before you were born. God is so good!
4. Expect God to do great things in our life! Look for miracles.
5. Be mindful of your tongue. Once you speak, hurtful words can't be taken back.
6. Enjoy a beautiful sunset or sunrise, it's God's artistry, His way of painting His way into our hearts.
7. Tell your child something you really like about them.
8. Pray for the disgruntled driver on the road, pray he makes it home.
9. Be thankful 1000 times plus a day. We can never be thankful enough.
10. You are loved more than you know, by someone who died to know you.

But God shows and clearly proves His [own] love for us by the fact that while we were still sinners, Christ (the Messiah, the Anointed One) died for us. Romans 5:8

HOW'S YOUR DAY GOING TO BE?

DO YOU KNOW you are special? In God's eyes, you are. Don't underestimate how you see yourself – you are so important to everyone around you – even those you have yet to meet. God has an amazing plan for your life – All you have to do is believe and trust in Him.

The plan is already laid out – just imagine, all you have to do is trust and He'll direct your path. Wow! That's pretty amazing – just like you! He thought you were so amazing, He died for you to set you free. Clean slate and grace upon grace. You are special! You are part of His kingdom. He has really great plans, don't you want to see what they are? Ask for Him to show you the way.

Kiss the Son [pay homage to Him in purity], lest He be angry and you perish in the way, for soon shall His wrath be kindled. O blessed (happy, fortunate, and to be envied) are all those who seek refuge and put their trust in Him. Psalm 2:12

HEAVEN SENT

If only for a moment,
you could see how truly beautiful you are
through Jesus' eyes.
All the imperfections you see
would then be cast outward to the sea.
They'd float around on the sea foam blue,
to bring you back to what you should already know.
You were Heaven sent, God adored,
now you shall cry, cry no more.
For it is He that sees you for who you are,
You are you, who He adores!
Selah.

[That you may really come] to know [practically, through experience for yourselves] the love of Christ, which far surpasses mere knowledge [without experience]; that you may be filled [through all your being] unto all the fullness of God [may have the richest measure of the divine Presence, and become a body wholly filled and flooded with God Himself]! Ephesians 3:19

ECHOES OF GOD

LORD, LET ME be an echo, where your words pierce my heart and fall from my lips at the beginning of every conversation. May the words I speak help calm and mend the broken hearts of strangers and friends.

May I speak eloquently on your behalf, and may they truly hear your words coming sweetly from my mouth.

May these words bathe them in compassion and soothe their souls.

May your kindness flow through me, so they may see and feel You, every time we meet. May they hear your voice echo through my words of truth, and may they have a longing so strong in their heart, that they want nothing more than to take refuge in You. Let me be an echo Lord, an echo that resonates your sweet voice and words everywhere I go.

I love you fervently and devotedly, O Lord, my Strength. The Lord is my rock, my Fortress, and my Deliverer; my God, my keen and firm Strength in Whom I will trust and take refuge, my Shield, and the Horn of my salvation, my High Tower. Psalm 18:1-2

TAKE FIVE TODAY

What's on today's calendar?

Work?

Doctor appointment?

Lunch appointment?

Kid's soccer, football, swim meet?

Church meeting?

Breathe … and take five minutes to be grateful to be alive in Him. Know it is He, who is the chauffeur of your heart. Take five today, and breath in His goodness. Take daily walks with Jesus. Plan your five moments with Him. Five moments today to just be:

Grateful

Praise Him

Refuel on His love

Breathe Him in

Live for Him.

INDESCRIBABLE LOVE

LET JESUS BE the chauffeur of your heart. Let Him be the "driver" of your thoughts and feelings. We live because of Him.

We love and worship Jesus, but how can you ever describe a love like His?

It truly is so beautiful, a fill up your heart kind of love. Words are hard to find to describe this love, lift up your arms and praise His name.

Let heaven (the angels) praise your wonders, O Lord, Your faithfulness also in the assembly of the holy ones (the holy angels). For who in the heavens can be compared to the Lord? Who among the mighty [heavenly beings] can be likened to the Lord. A God greatly feared and revered in the council of the holy (angelic) ones, and to be feared and worshipfully revered above all those who are around Him? O Lord God of hosts, who is a mighty one like unto You, O Lord? And your faithfulness is round about You [an essential part of You at all times]. Psalm 89:5-8.

THOUGHT BUBBLES

I DIDN'T WAKE up joyful, I woke up kind of cranky. I pause and remember Peter Pan – "think a happy thought," so I think of one, and another and another! I think about Jesus and what He's done for me, and the thought bubbles come faster and faster. In what seems like a millisecond I go from cranky pants to this giddy, little kid, because He is so amazing!

He loves us, and I find that unbelievable even in my cranky pants. I think of all He's done, how He moves, how He heals, how He saves, and my thoughts go off the charts. My cranky pants come off, and my wardrobe changes to joy. Beautiful joy takes over and my day transforms, my outlook changes and I stand and shout, "I LOVE YOU, LORD!" Thank you for loving me! You are my joy – And I find joy today between coffee, cranky pants and thought bubbles, and I smile and say – "Today shall be beautiful."

Think happy thoughts today, think Jesus. Shout it out ..."I love Jesus!"

Now, go out there, spread joy and have a beautiful, Sondrenched day!

BAND OF ANGELS

IN THE MIDST of navigating your journey through life, have faith. Your divine wisdom and light shine so brightly, and even though you may sense a flickering or uneven flame – believe in yourself. Know that God is sending a band of angels to rally on your behalf. These angels will lift you during your trials, your unknown days, and soon you'll see God's plan for you in all its glory. Your destiny on this planet is beautifully set to the beat, the beat of God's heart and yours entwined through eternity.

Set the seeds of life in motion, sprinkle gently, and God will help these seeds grow into a magical garden for you to watch grow. Know that your life is God-breathed.

Take time for yourself, have compassion for your circumstances and know that the changes you seek are already within you. Focus on what inspires you and brings you joy. You are one of the brightest lights on this planet. God will help you find your way through the shifting tides. Have faith in Him, but most of all have faith in yourself.

But to as many as did receive and welcome Him, He gave the authority (power, privilege, right) to become the children of God, that is, to those who believe in (adhere to, trust in, and rely on) His name. John 1:12

RAY OF HOPE

MAY THESE WORDS be a delicate enchanting reminder, of God's love for you and who you've become in Him. Let's draw nearer, inhale His beauty, and on the exhale shout, "Yes, You are my treasured Lord! You may carry me through the storms of my life!"

I will surpass all that is to be, for You are the light at the end of the path You set before me.

Forgive us our doubt, as we inhale knowing You know our every heartbeat, every joy and every fear. Let our exhales be the pressure reliever, the deal breaker that You Lord, have indeed marked our hearts as yours!

May your day be filled with Sonshine. May you slow down and inhale every intricate detail of this day. May you never forget the infamous day when the gentle coos of a new baby announced His own arrival by crying out, "I am the King of all Kings, the Lord of all Lords, The Messiah, born to save, born to love You.

Amen

CONNECTIONS TO GOD

AS I AGE I grumble for I no longer look the same. When I see lines rise up on my face, I know exactly where I was, and I'm reminded of where I am now. Each line is my connection to God where I called Him closer, where I cried out in pain. I love these lines, and when I see them I know I found unconditional love. May you find beauty in the mirror, God's mirror, where our reflection is pure perfection because we are made new in Him.

"Lord, teach us to love ourselves as You love us. May our sons and daughters see a difference in us and who we are in Christ."

May we as parents, teach our children to not rely on society to tell them who they are; if they know they are loved by Jesus, then they can rely on him, and they will gain freedom and self-confidence. It's what our Heavenly Father sees in us, undying love for us where every line on our face is His love line, where we cried out to Him. Love lines where He cuddled us and wrapped us in His blanket of compassion and protection. He has kept us safe, telling us we are beautifully made only by Him. It is the assurance that we are loved more than we will ever know by someone who died to know us.

I will confess and praise You for You are fearful and wonderful and for that awful wonder of my birth! Wonderful are Your works, and that my inner self knows right well. Psalm 139:14

REACH FOR THE SON

WHERE DO YOU go to pray? Do you have a quiet spot? I found this massive oak tree where I like to go and pray. Sometimes we seek out the solitude of an area that brings peace to our soul; this tree does this for me.

This oak tree is magnificent as it ages with grace. The trunk of this tree is so large, and the bark has many intricate lines and ridges showing it has weathered many storms. Growth and aging are inevitable in this lifetime. This grand oak is aging, and it's clear it is thriving, as its roots are firmly planted keeping it strong and stable. It thrives as it reaches for the Son! This tree protects many birds and small animals from the elements, and also gives shade and peace to those who choose to remain under its blanket of protection.

Today, choose to remain under Jesus' blanket of protection, by planting your faith strongly in Him. Relying on Jesus will help you grow stronger, as His grace rains down on you. He will nourish your soul with His love, His strength will bring you through the storms in life. Reach for the Son, allow Him to nourish and fulfill your needs. Pray for peace for your soul today.

And He shall be like a tree firmly planted [and tended] by the streams of water, ready to bring forth its fruit in its season; its leaf also shall not fade or wither; and everything he does shall prosper [and come to maturity]. Psalm 1:3

I'D RATHER NOT!

THEIR LIFE WAS unhappy, so they bought stuff ... electronics, clothes, cars and such ... and they filled their lives and told their neighbors their jobs were not what they expected and neither was their life. When it came time to help the man down the street they passed him by, unaware that by picking him up he would have been saved by them! When their time had come, they left behind assorted possessions that their children couldn't wait to receive, yet no one cared that they were gone!

IMPACT: They left nothing! No happiness, no shine, only selfishness that they passed onto their children. Was their life worth it, to never have helped a single soul, only to feed their hunger for selfishness? What a way to live ... I'd rather not. I'd rather be remembered as owning nothing, having nothing, yet having everything in the lives I helped along the way. I'd rather be remembered for living my life for Christ!

Do not gather and heap up and store up for yourselves treasures on earth, where moth and rust and worm consume and destroy, and where thieves break through and steal. But gather and heap up and store for yourselves treasures in heaven, where neither moth nor rust nor worm consume and destroy, and where thieves do not break through and steal; For where your treasure is, there will your heart be also. Matthew 6:19-21

ALWAYS HOME

I WENT HOME to the house I grew up in. A silence fell on the house, and as the midnight mist rolled in I noticed everything looked so small. Tiny furniture that fits my 4'11" mother who longs for days gone by. Do you long for your past or look to the future? Do you feel you are ever so small in God's eyes? Home is what you make it, the love, God's love and how you embrace your life. Content in who you are in Christ, and living life with a Christ heart, leads you to where He needs you to be. We are oh so small, on a big planet that needs to hear of Jesus love. He's a big God, and we are not small in His eyes. We are His. No boundaries or miles keep us apart. He waits for us to come to Him, He calls us from the door to our future. Paths laid out by Him and His glorious plans all await us, as He yearns for us to come back to what we know. God is our Home in our heart – No yearning for the past as His plans for our future call us forward. It is up to us to leap. He has wondrous plans for our lives, and trusting in Him to put these plans in motion will challenge us to leave behind what we know. God is so good, yet His plans for our life are inconceivable – until we ultimately allow Him to show us the Big Plan. The bravest move forward, the smallest take steps, and He looks on at us with adoring eyes. One God, one big love, and your heart become home wherever you may be.

In all of your ways know, recognize, and acknowledge Him, and He will direct and make straight and plain your paths. Proverbs 3:6

WHISPER OF LOVE

AS THE SUN stretches its light across the world waking us up to a new day, You are here, Lord. We hear your whispers of love as the trees gently move to and fro.

Oh my Lord, how You love us, and without a doubt, your love fills our souls with a newness, only You can provide. Keep the enchantment and brilliance of this new day in us, as we awaken refreshed from our evening's slumber. We will glorify You, and see your wonder in every little corner of our world as You gently remind us You are here.

Selah, we pause and realize, it is You who loves us. You are here Lord, giving us life and breath, and we thank You for your Son. Selah We pause and know this love will never end. You are here with us always. Selah! We breathe in this stunning day as You paint the sky with a multitude of colors and brilliance. Your sunrise is our constant reminder that You live in us. We praise You for this brand new day.

This is the day which the Lord as brought about; we will rejoice and be glad in it. Psalm 118:24

THE HANDS OF TIME

THE HANDS OF time kept ticking on and on, as she waited with anxious anticipation. Every day at the crack of dawn she'd rise up and pray with the rooster's crow. At the moment the cock-a-doodle-do hit the highest of notes, her mountain of expectancy in His answering her prayer became her mountain of hope!

Maybe not today, maybe not tomorrow, but she knew when He was ready God would answer. So, she prayed with high hopes each morning and night for Him to answer, but each day the prayer changed. Each day her hope grew, and on that day when He answered her prayer, she knew He had given her the greatest answer to prayer she could ever hope for. As she watched the sunrise and the rooster crow, the mountain on the horizon seemed to shrink as it kissed the sunrise.

Jesus, her sweet Redeemer taught her to believe in Him. As she prayed daily, she never faltered in her faith. HE WAS HER GOD. He held the key to her heart! He knew what the road looked like ahead. Her prayers changed because her faith grew in Him. She relied on Him to answer!

She still prays by the mountainside. The rooster has grown old and his crows are long gone, but her prayers are always answered in His time, and she knows His love will never cease, for she hopes in Him.

Praised (honored, blessed) be the God and Father of our Lord Jesus Christ (the Messiah)! By His boundless mercy we have been born again to an ever living hope through the resurrection of Jesus Christ from the dead. 1 Peter 1:3

HE'S YOUR AUTHOR!

I LOOKED AT my computer keyboard and focused on this ... as you "enter" into today's activities, how much are you still trying to "control?" Do you go "up and down" in your day, second guessing yourself? Does it seem like you are always going "back and forth" with decisions?

Decide today to "insert" God into all your decisions. Ask for guidance, and He will "delete" the indecision, and put in your heart what is clear and concise, no more "backspaces" needed!

With God as the "author" of your life, things will become easier, and as you "shift" directions giving Him control, your path will take on new meaning. He is the way and the truth! Living with God more deeply planted in your heart, allows you to grow to new depths of understanding. The misdirected will be directed to joy. Let Him "edit" out where change is needed!

For from Him and through Him and to Him are all things. [For all things originate with Him and come from Him; all things live through Him, and all things center in and tend to consummate and to end in Him.] To Him be glory forever! Amen (so be it). Romans 11:36

DON'T WORRY

IF YOU LOOK back on your life, how much time have you spent worrying? How much time have you lost? Did it change the outcome? God can release you from worry. He already knows the troubles ahead of us. He also sees our brilliant futures. If you talk to anyone about your worries, talk to God.

He doesn't promise a worry-free life. He doesn't promise nothing bad will happen. He does promise He will protect us and help us find joy in Him. Trust in Him.

Don't lose countless hours and beautiful moments of your life on worry. Imagine a jar that you place every single worry in. How big is the jar? Is it overflowing with worry, or is it hardly filled at all? Imagine if you trust in God, how full do you think the jar will be? No jar is needed! He knows all of our worries, He carries all of our worries and tears in His jar. We have a choice, fill up our jar or His, which will you choose? Choose Him to carry you through.

But seek (aim at and strive after) first of all His kingdom and His righteousness (His way of doing and being right), and then all these things taken together will be given you besides. So do not worry or be anxious about tomorrow, for tomorrow will have worries and anxieties of its own. Sufficient for each day is its own trouble. Matthew 6:33-34.

THE PATHS OF MY SOUL

WHEN I FEEL God walk up and down the paths to my soul, I feel a peace like never before. I have traveled many paths without Him, some have been rocky, some have been dark, but the paths I am most fond of are the paths that I have walked with Him. These are the paths where I have found my greatest peace and calm after the storm.

We never travel alone, for He is always taking this life journey with us. He paves the way on the path of our journey in life, one brick at a time.

Cause me to hear Your loving kindness in the morning, for on You do I lean and in You do I trust. Cause me to know the way wherein I should walk, for I lift up my inner self to You. Psalm 143:8

YOUR EPIC LIFE

YOU CAN CHANGE your life today! You can sit and wallow, or you can pray "God will you move in my life today?" You can cry, or you can come to prayer with hands folded and say "God I can't do this alone, I need You." Fear is a liar. Worry holds us back from living the life God intended for us. All things are possible with God. Let go, let God, for He has plans not to harm you, but to help you prosper. Do you want power? Ask God to move in your life, give Him the power to change your life – You are capable of having an epic life with God if you are willing to work for it and let Him work and move for you.

Jump in - The waters of life are waiting – Let Him drench you in His peace.

And God, Who is acquainted with and understands the heart, bore witness to them, giving them the Holy Spirit as He also did to us. And He made no difference between us and them, but cleansed their hearts by faith (by a strong and welcome conviction that Jesus is the Messiah, through whom we obtain eternal salvation in the kingdom of God). Acts 15:8-9

I PRAY

I Pray for patience – I am still waiting.

I Pray for love – I found You, God.

I Pray for pain to cease – You give me sleep, Lord.

I Pray for strength – Lord You give me endurance.

I Pray for healing – Little by little You heal me, Lord.

I Pray for friends – You teach me to trust.

I Pray for my parents – They call laughing.

I Pray for my children – My Heart is Full.

You are a good, good Father, and your love, kindness, healing and understanding never ceases. I live for You – because of You, my citizenship in heaven is guaranteed!

Selah

But we are citizens of the state (commonwealth, homeland) which is in heaven, and from it also we earnestly and patiently await [the coming of] the Lord Jesus Christ (the Messiah) [as] Savior. Philippians 3:20

JOY METER

SOMETIMES OUR "JOY meter" gets stuck between this moment and the next. I was told to find gratitude today, and my joy would find itself. I woke up achy and just not myself. I needed coffee, lots of coffee. So, I dumped the beans into the grinder and the earth-shaking sound of beans on metal challenges me to wake up. I add water, and patiently wait for my first cup of coffee as the coffee slowly drips into the carafe. Why is it when you are desperately in need of a caffeine fix, the coffee pot seems to take forever? I skip the mug and pour the milk directly into the pot, and I chug it down. The carafe feels large in my hand, and I realize it feels like today will be a "nothing-seems-to-fit" kind of day. Now, I can go about my business all day and believe that nothing will fit, or I can try to fill my world with thoughts of gratitude. I decide to not get caught up in the moment of "Life is just not fair!"

I go to work and I see tiny love notes from God spread out along my path. I can't seem to open them because I am still too tired and worn out. It's in this moment I realize this tired feeling can make you more tired if you allow yourself to resonate on just how tired you truly are.

Today is a ho-hum day and my "joy meter" is still stuck on empty. I sit and ponder, what is it going to take to get my joy meter back up? Nine o'clock melts into ten o'clock, and I'm still stuck in the moment of just being tired. I take a break and go for a walk. As I walk outside the sun melts through me, and I can feel myself soaking up the rays. Suddenly, I become Son drenched in the beauty of the day! I allow God to light my path, and I absorb all that He is trying to show me. I sit on a bench, and as the sun bathes me in wonder, I hear a gentle tapping from the left. I look up and there in the old oak tree is a giant woodpecker, larger than any woodpecker I've ever seen. He's banging his beak into the bark of the tree trying to find the goodness inside the trunk. This bird is not stopping until he finds it! I can almost feel the impact of his beak as he tries over and over, to break through to the core.

Suddenly it hits me! God has been trying all morning to get my attention, banging and tapping on my brain sending love signals, and I wasn't noticing. I wasn't listening! I almost missed it, but this beauty of a woodpecker was my saving grace who reminded me, "Stop trying to do it all, let go and let God." He sees potential in all you do, and He wants nothing more than for you to know, He loves you! As this woodpecker, this tiny love note from God hopped around the tree, I became so grateful and my "joy meter" shot to total joy.

You have said, Seek My face [inquire for and require My presence as your vital need]. My heart says to You, Your face (Your presence), Lord, will I seek, inquire for, and require [of necessity and on the authority of Your Word]. Psalm 27:8

HE IS

EVEN IN THE midst of our crazy day, He listens to our prayers. Lean in close today – You are boldly and amazingly created by the ultimate Creator Himself. Wherever you are today, whatever you are called to do, you can, but not because of your awesomeness! Oh, there is no doubt you are amazingly made, but what you do, you do because HE IS! He is awesome, and you were created in His image for His purpose. For His glory and by His Grace. You can do hard things, and beautiful things today. You are His image bearer – Shine like the Son! Be blessed because you are a blessing to others, no matter what He created you to do. Inspire others today – Have a blessed day in Him.

Make today the day you inspire others to be followers of Christ. I just want you to know, He thinks you are some kind of special!

And it was of His own [free] will that He gave us birth [as sons] by [His] Word of Truth, so that we should be a kind of firstfruits of His creatures [a sample of what He created to be consecrated to Himself]. James 1:18

ACTIVATE YOUR POWER

THERE IS A power within you that exceeds any human emotion tenfold.

This power is faith!

Faith in God.

Faith in yourself.

Faith in family and friends.

Faith in mankind.

When you unleash this power and have faith that God has you, this power can raise you to new levels. Faith in God's plan for your life without seeing His plan exceeds any purpose you have preconceived in your mind. God's will, God's way. Ultimately, when you activate your faith and rise up to believing anything is possible with God, this is when your purpose shall be revealed. Activate your faith! Believe in His plan. He is mightier than any plan you have laid out. When you ask Him to activate this plan, jump. Life will take a new turn and ultimately, God moments will be displayed tenfold in your life. Have faith. Activate.

Thank you, God, for giving us the Holy Spirit as a guarantee of the fulfillment of Your promise in our lives.

Sonset

The beauty of the evening, as the sun kisses the Earth, can only be brought to you by the greatest artist of our time, God himself.

GOD'S SERENADE

THERE'S THIS SERENITY on my porch in the evening darkness. The world comes alive with the chatter of crickets calling in unison to the world. The cricket song requests sleep for one and all. Tree frogs are singing, and God's small creatures call out to Him one by one, singing their love song in harmony. This evening is an enchanting reminder of God's love for us. Off in the distance, the hoot owl is calling loud and clear "Jesus come, "our Jesus come." The hoot owl knows what the world needs, rock-a-byes and the gentle wonder of God's love in the sounds of His tiny creatures who never stop serenading all night long. The Earth is calling to God, and His gentle whispers echo through the trees, "Be still and know I Am. Be still and know I Am your God." This gentle reminder calms the Earth as Jesus draws nearer on this enchanting evening only He can orchestrate.

Rest well, and know your God is with you, and all is well with our souls.

Let be and be still, and know(recognize and understand) that I am God. I will be exalted among the nations! I will be exalted in the Earth! Psalm 46:10

HE EVENS IT OUT

YOU KNOW, IT'S really hard to put it in perspective sometimes, hard to humble ourselves enough to say, "God, I can't do this thing. You know all this stuff in my heart." So we inhale and on the exhale, He captures our exasperation from the events of the day, and it evens everything out when He sends us evening bliss.

Hearts beating wildly from a chaotic day come to a calming halt on His command, because He holds everyone's heart in His hand. He has our heart in His grasp. Like a calming, crisp dive in a pool of crystal blue, He's there catching us and not allowing us to fall.

Lean on, trust in, and be confident in the Lord with all your heart and mind and do not rely on your own insight or understanding. Proverbs 3:5.

ENCHANTING GRACE

I LOOK AT the beautiful grass-lined edge of my world as it slips up to greet the evening sunset. Green to red, pink and gray, and the colors offset the beauty of the sun laying down for the evening. I embrace the enchanting grace, as silence stills the echoes coming from the hillside. The cricket song hushes the wind, and the evenings first minutes graciously come. Dusk turns to darkness as I lift up your life to God. I know He hears me. I know in this hope-filled evening your life journey is in its finest hours.

You are so loved by Jesus. I ask the angels to gently fly be and fill you deeply with the Holy Spirit. Thy will be done I sing, as I know your finest days are yet to come! He's never left your side, and I call Him to watch over you as this new evening unfolds.

Your time has come for His undying love to wrap you in His care and devotion. As He shifts the day into night the moon sleepily awakens. I know in the midst of this beautiful evening, God has a specific plan for you. People look at you in amazement. They will see God's handiwork unravel, and we will all know you are His finest child, full of Grace. I hear His voice gently whisper, "my child it will be all right. He who is constantly in motion with me shall shine like the sun of a new day." As the man in the moon pulls up his evening blanket, and the tree frogs lullaby tucks us in, I know your days will be blessed and you shall indeed shine, for God has made it so! Selah

PERFECT PEACE

LORD, ON THIS stellar starlit evening we are amazingly in love with You. We are crazy in love with your grace and blessings. You always have the timing down to the precise minute to capture our weary, aching hearts. You seize our day with your lovely way of infusing our souls with love and your touch of love.

I saw your handiwork in the cloud formations tonight as the sun sizzled on the horizon. You reached for me, and like a tiny child lost in a magical world of Legos, You found that "perfect piece," that perfect piece of your heart and made me swoon for You.

May your heart swoon for Him tonight! May you find Him in the corners of your heart and be mesmerized by His amazing love. May you become crazy in love with Him as He sets a fire in your heart.

O give thanks to the Lord, for He is good; for His Mercy and loving-kindness endure forever! Psalm 107:1

THE NINE GIFTS

I WALKED INTO the room, and there sat nine gifts. There was a note attached saying, "Give these away," teach others." So, I gathered them up and handed them out like hot pretzels from the street vendor in New York City. As each gift was opened, I saw lives transformed! The first was for a woman crying and all alone, the gift was LOVE. The second gift I gave to an unhappy man. I gave him JOY. The third gift I gave to a soldier riddled with PTSD, this gift was the one I treasured. This gift is PEACE. The fourth gift I gave to an angry mom yelling at her child, I gave her PATIENCE. The fifth gift I gave to the young woman who had lost her way, I gave her FAITHFULNESS. I stood there for a bit wondering who would receive the last of my gifts. I looked over into the dog park and I saw a man beating his dog, I ran over and gave him the sixth gift of GENTLENESS, he never beat his dog again!

I came across a young couple screaming at each other in rage, I gave them the seventh gift of SELF-CONTROL. They opened the package slowly and as they did, a great appreciation for each other came over them, and they stopped yelling! I gave the eight gift to a man who had just lost his wife, his gift was THE GOODNESS IN GOD, and he slowly found his way back to Jesus.

The ninth gift I gave to myself, it means so much to me. I gave myself KINDNESS. It's a gift to be shared, and I pass it around, and as I do, I also give the gift of kindness to you. Share kindness and watch your world change.

But the fruit of the [Holy] Spirit [the work which His presence within accomplishes] is love, joy (gladness), peace, patience (an even temper, forbearance), kindness, goodness benevolence), faithfulness. Gentleness (meekness, humility), self-control (self-restraint, continence). Against such things there is no law [that can bring change]. If we live by the [Holy] Spirit, let us also walk by the Spirit. [If by the Holy Spirit we have our life in God, let us go forward walking in line, our conduct controlled by the Spirit.] Galatians 5:22-25

BRILLIANT LIGHT

DAY TURNS TO night as wispy clouds float on by. Darkness has settled in as Jesus' brilliant light reflects in the night sky. Gentle, puffy clouds remind me of His embrace, and I hear "I Am here!" Sweet Jesus, I long for the day when I feel your closeness in every beat of my heart, every breath I take. I've come to a crossroads in my life, where the chaos of the world engulfs me like an ocean tide, and I don't know what to do. The struggles of the day linger into the night like a fog trying to lure me to another place. In the sky where the clouds softness reminds me of You, I remain. I drink in the beauty of the evening as the cricket song gently lures me into a peaceful state. I hear your whisper, "I am here." Take me back, Lord. Take my heart to the place where your love gently caresses my heart like the ocean tide caresses the shoreline. Take my heart, Lord, and turn it to you. I long for You, yet this day plays over and over in my mind. Calm my mind, Lord and help me to remember the hush of silence where I am so in tune with You. The darkness has come, and with it, there's this longing for your soul-drenching silence where I only hear your calming whispers, and the world gets drowned out. I call to You, and You come running – Take me back, Lord, to where I need to be, where I long to be, undone by You.

And God said to Moses, I AM WHO I AM, and WHAT I AM, and I WILL BE WHAT I WILL BE; and He said, You shall say this to the Israelites; I AM sent me to you! Exodus 3:14

MIDNIGHT PRAYER

LORD, BLESS US as we sleep tonight. Fill us with peace and the love of your heart. Fill us, rejuvenate us to have the energy to fulfill your legacy of kindness and a soul that walks amongst the broken. Instill in us a kind heart to know when it's best for us to walk away. Guard our hearts against the enemy, and keep all doors closed where it is unsafe for us to walk. We love You Father, and there is no other way to love but to love through You. May we walk this Earth as You once did, laying hands on those who need healing prayers and a kind heart.

Help us to love our children as You love us with a gentleness so they can continue to grow into loving, kind souls. Father, your love is like a gentle breeze which allows the eagle to fly mighty and proud. May You always hear our voices call You our Beloved because we love You more than life itself. Live on in us, Your will be done.

Amen.

HE'S OUR RESTFUL NIGHT

THERE'S THIS HUSH that comes at nightfall when rest is ready but our hearts need calming from a day of wannabes, do-overs, and just plain soul-seeking bliss. Tomorrow will come, and with it a clean slate to get back up and do the really hard things again.

The crickets chirping and tree frogs singing in perfect harmony, are serenading Jesus up above. As Jesus gets ready to tuck us all in for the night, listen for His whisper, listen for the wonder of it all. He didn't spend time hanging on the cross for us to just muddle through our days. He grants us brilliance that shines through our cracked open hearts. Listen, and you'll hear Him say, "I am. I am your silence at night. I am your brilliance by day. I am your comforter and peace. I AM."

As the tree frogs and crickets amp up their love song in unison, He's our rest at night, and our storm calmer by day. "Sleep tight," He whispers, "I AM right here!"

And they who know Your name [who have experience and acquaintance with Your Mercy] will lean on and confidently put their trust in You, for You Lord, have not forsaken those who seek (inquire of and for) You [on the authority of God's Word and the right of necessity] Psalm 9:10

HEART BEATS

Inhale, Exhale … Repeat

INHALE confidence.

EXHALE doubt.

INHALE wisdom.

EXHALE hesitation.

INHALE God's Grace.

EXHALE love.

INHALE beauty.

EXHALE brilliance.

INHALE God's love.

EXHALE peace.

Repeat …

Then Jesus said to them again, Peace to you! [Just] as the Father has sent Me forth, so I am sending you. And having said this, He breathed on them and said to them, Receive the Holy Spirit. John 20:21-22

SOFTLY, YOU CALL ME

As the fluffy, pink clouds whisk on by bidding the sun its final farewell, I hear your voice and I see Your glory! Teach me to listen, Lord, to slow down and hear You amongst the ripples at the water's edge.

Softly, You call my name through the eagle's cry as I watch him fly overhead. I am reminded of your love as the brilliant red sun starts to sizzle and fall from the sky. Even through the darkness of the evening, You are here!

Teach me to see how You are in every particle, every intricate detail of nature's grace. You paint a picture in the early evening sky, and your love shines through the reds and purples swirling in the sunset of my life. I listen and hear another day gracefully carried off into the night. I praise You for all You are and all You give me. I hear You Lord, and my heart sings an enchanting love song through the night … I am free.

Selah.

HIS SPIRIT WITHIN US

REMEMBER, WHEN WE long to hear God speak, He is more than language and words. He's more than feelings formed in the human heart. He is a God of experiences. He loves to experience life with us. When He died, His spirit stayed to be within us.

Speech is translated through the language of our hearts. We need to trust Him when He puts things in our hearts. We need to do what He puts in our hearts. God's heart is not silent, He loves us too much to not communicate through our hearts. He wants us to know and feel who we are in Him.

And He said to them, When you pray, say: Our Father Who is in Heaven, hallowed be Your name, Your kingdom come, Your will be done [held holy and revered] on Earth as it is in heaven. Give us our bread [food for the morrow]. And forgive us our sins, for we ourselves also forgive everyone who is indebted to us [who has offended us or done wrong]. And bring us not into temptation but rescue us from evil. Luke 11:2-4

WAIT FOR IT

WHEN YOU TOUCH the corners of the Earth, when you raise your hands to Jesus and there is silence, wait for it. When you try to hear Him and it is silent, wait for it. He's working. His clock is sometimes slower than time itself, yet He's working! Working in you, for you and all around you. Just wait for Him.

Even though it seems as if time is standing still, and you feel the time is wasted or running out, wait for Him. Wait on Him. Wait on God!

Like the sun that bathes your skin on a sunlit day, wait on Him. While you blissfully lay on the sand, and hear the ocean waves dancing on the shoreline, wait on Him.

He will appear at the corners of the Earth and seek you out for your calling.

But you, beloved, build yourselves up [founded] on your most holy faith [make progress, rise like an edifice higher and higher], praying in the Holy Spirit. Guard and keep yourselves in the love of God; expect and patiently wait for the mercy of the Lord Jesus Christ the (Messiah) – [which will bring you] unto life eternal. Jude 1:20-21

YET TO COME

FATHER GOD, YAHWEH, we need You tonight and always. You are our Alpha and Omega, our One and Only! We hear your soft whispers of, "I AM" echoing through the mountain tops. All that is and was, we call on You for You are our Yet to Come.

We hold your hand tonight, we feel your presence. You, our Heavenly Father are in control of our destiny. We desire and feel You drawing nearer tonight. Lord wrap us up tight, as tight as when Mary wrapped Jesus in swaddling clothes. Tonight we become childlike with an essence of no more fear, strength beyond strength and with childlike eyes, we believe what we can't see. We believe with our hearts, Father God. Your power is so significant – Help us to light up our world and shine your light from city to city announcing, "We are your children, and You Father, shall rein forever." We hope in You. We feel You tonight – Yahweh, we love You like never before! Strong like Your Son's love, shine on us, wrap Your arms around us and let our world find peace, nothing but love in our world.

Selah – We pause to breathe You in and on the exhale we know, we are loved beyond measure. Selah and hallelujah, we are reborn in You!

CHERISHED BY GOD

SAY THIS TO yourself over and over tonight, as you sleepily fall into slumber.

I am deeply loved.

I am divinely appointed.

I am abundantly equipped.

And I am cherished by God.

No plan of Satan or obstacle can keep me from God's highest and best will for my life. As I follow the voice of my Jesus, I can see the invisible, accomplish the impossible and love the unlovable. I am a living, breathing miracle because Jesus Christ lives in me!

Amen.

For we are God's [own] handiwork His workmanship) recreated in Christ Jesus, [born anew] that we may do those good works which God predestined planned beforehand) for us [taking paths which He prepared ahead of time], that we should walk in them [living the good life which He prearranged and made ready for us to live]. Ephesians 2:10

UNDO ME LORD

I SAT THERE staring at the beads, broken and falling from my necklace onto my nightstand. It was like an explosion had rained down from my head! Almost as if all the blessings from my day, every single one that I had been granted had spilled out of my memory bank and fell right in front of me.

What had I forgotten today? What had I left behind that had gotten me so unraveled on this day? I had left Jesus' side, and I became entangled in a web of chaos! I stopped right there next to my bedside, staring at the beads as they came to a complete stop and I began to pray ...

Undo me, Lord! As this day unraveled and my thoughts started to wander, forgive me, Father. Undo, me Lord. Settle in, calm my heart and take me back to what I know, take me back to the serenity of You. Help me to see that today didn't have to be a day of unraveling, but could have been a day of brilliance, straightened out because of You. Today I did hard things. Tomorrow will be much of the same, but Lord, Undo me. Calm my heart and bring me back to what I know, what I long for, what I yearn for ... You! Undo me, Lord. Help me find my way back to you. Amen

BLESSED AND SAVED BY HIM

I SAT ON the edge of my bed as a calmness came over me, and I knew in that moment God is always faithful. If we rely on Him, we won't become unraveled.

Tonight is the night! Drop off the "shout outs" from people who don't believe in you. Drop them at the foot of the cross. Drop off the doubt, mistrust and every other label you've allowed yourself to believe. Show the one true King you live for Him. When you are feeling like this day is the last day you want to crawl out of bed, and you long to be someone else, remember I AM. Because He lives in you, YOU CAN.

When you feel like you don't have the strength, HE CAN carry you through your day into the evening. When you've expelled all your energy on the thoughts in your head, HE WILL calm your mind and soul. HE IS the one true King, and YOU are part of His kingdom of believers. He knows tonight you are tired. Give it up to Him, and HE WILL carry you through to tomorrow.

You are a beautiful soul redeemed by Him. Remain in Him tonight, seek joy, truth and find His everlasting love. Show the "shouters" of this world, who you are.

Blessed and saved by Him.

God is our Refuge and Strength [mighty and impenetrable to temptation], a very present and well-proved help in trouble. Psalm 46:1

PRAYERS FOR THE BROKEN

FATHER, WE PRAISE You for this day. Your glory has shown us in intricate detail all of our blessings. We count each one as a "love note" from You. This evening as we lay down for a peaceful rest, we ask that You grant us pain-free sleep. Come, sit and watch over us. We seek your presence in the stillness of the night, as the tree frogs gently sing enchantingly beautiful melodies in the background of our evening.

We lift up those who hurt, who desperately need and long for healing. Place your hand on those who are weary, and breathe peace deep into their souls. We know you're in control of our lives, our beautiful days and evenings too. Draw in closer Lord, set a flame in us that burns bright. Show us your vision for our lives. We know your plans for us are not to harm us, to not let us fall. We know You are here right now leading us to our Eden, our place of rest and tranquility. With You, all things are possible Lord. Amp up our faith and fill the voids in our heart with joy, the joy of having a more intimate relationship with You.

May we rise tomorrow knowing You carry us through our day. We will keep our eyes on You, Lord, as our love for You grows stronger each and every day!

Amen.

PRAYER WARRIORS

LORD, I'M ASKING for your soul healing, your downright heart mending touch for all of those who have chosen the Prayer Warrior path. Your warriors are so loyal, work so hard for You with no questions, no expectations other than joy felt love and devotion to You. Bless the warriors as they bring your message of love to those in need.

Give special healing to the hearts of the worn and weary, as they give of their selves to others bringing your word to the needy and broken. Let them know that it's your plan for them to take a rest from their everyday work. Allow them to find solitude in your love for them. Please, give them rest and allow the joy to flow back into their hearts. Give them strength for tomorrow, to have the best day and to be able to share their love with those around them. Allow them to refuel and drench their selves in You.

Allow them to feel the love of other prayer warriors as it is meant to be when others pray together. Set their hearts on fire each and every day. Help them to rise up so those in need can see You through them.

Bless the prayer warriors as they continue on into their week drawing others closer to you, Lord.

Amen.

LAY IT ALL DOWN

IN THE MIDST of this beautiful evening, we lay down all our thoughts and problems. You know Lord, the stuff we carry like old luggage on a trip to the utmost corners of our minds. Lord, our hearts become so heavy at times, help us to remember to lay it all down at the Cross. This is where our burdens are lifted and our travels become joyous.

Heal those who are sick, and give rest to those who are weary.

We praise You for the light You shine so brightly on all of us. We lift up those who are working so hard to shine your light on others.

Grant us a restful, peaceful evening.

Bless those who will be caring for sick family members or friends. Give those who need it most healing hands and compassionate hearts.

We praise You, Lord, for our beautiful lives, and for sending us Your Son who gives us such grace.

Amen.

Again He said to him the second time, Simon, son of John, do you love Me [with reasoning, intentional, spiritual devotion, as one loves the Father]? He said to Him, Yes, Lord, You know that I love You [that I have a deep, instinctive, personal affection for You, as for a close friend]. He said to him, Shepherd tend) My sheep. John 21:16

TICKET TO ETERNITY

SAY, "AH," AND be in awe of how Jesus has brought you through this day. Mountains to climb hurdles to jump or smooth sailing, He's right there. He never leaves. He's like a vacation that never ends. He carries your baggage as you breeze through the checkpoints of your day running to your next destination in your life. He runs with you because He adores you!

Grab your ticket - His ticket to eternity never expires! His beauty and the serenity of this day can be yours, just ask and He delivers bountiful bliss and Son-filled days.

May you always remain in His presence, may you look up and be grateful for His refreshing peace. He's right there with you – Take a mini vacation tonight in prayer and gratitude. Find your comfort and relaxing bliss in Him.

Even to your old age I am He, and even to hair white with age will I carry you. I have made, and I will bear; yes, I will carry and will save you. Isaiah 46:4

LIQUID GRACE

HAVE YOU TOUCHED God today, or did He touch you? As you sit in silence under the Son, did you feel His touch on your heart? I want to move through this life with liquid grace. Liquid grace where tears may flow at times, but He's there to catch them. He lifts our spirit to a higher dimension where we will see no flaws in others, just God's face on everyone we touch - that's God-given grace.

He's calling us to a higher dimension, calling us to become who He intended us to be. What is your calling? Have you melted into His liquid grace so you may flow with Him? Have you felt His touch in your life today, or have you touched Him with your devotion? Pray for Him to flow through you like liquid grace.

These moments where He sings to us, loves us and fills us up with so much grace and admiration, are our affirmation that we are gliding and dancing with Him through life. Dance with Him today as He touches your heart, allow yourself to melt into Him. You are already amazing. Let Jesus' love shine through and let His love flow.

Through Him also we have [our] access entrance, introduction) by faith into this grace state of God's favor) in which we [firmly and safely] stand. And let us rejoice and exult in our hope of experiencing and enjoying the glory of God. Romans 5:2

BLANKET OF LOVE

LORD, WE ARE here in final wait. We wait for You to bring all the world's troubles to rest. We ask You to surround our planet with a blanket of love, a blanket that changes everything and removes the hatred from the souls of those who haven't found You. Help those who are lost to find your kind heart and peace. Surround our world with a ray beam from your heart. May they be Son drenched realizing that no matter what color skin we may have, we all are born of You. May we all find it in our hearts to stop the hatred and instill in us a strong love where we find our joy. May You blanket the Earth, the universe with a love song for all to hear. You are the only one Lord who can bring this magical essence of harmony to our planet. Bring back the rhythm that flows gracefully with the rotation of our planet, a planet that needs Jesus and loves without judgment. Help us to love with open arms like you do.

Amen.

And whatever you ask for in prayer, having faith and [really] believing, you will receive. Matthew 21:22

PRAYER OF INTERCEDING

LORD, MY GOD how I love thee. You fill me up with love when I need it most. When the world's troubles drag me down, there you are leaving me in total amazement. You check on the broken, You heal those that are torn, torn between two places in time that only You can comprehend. Those missing loved ones.

I lift up my family and friends. I ask that You fill them with peace on this magnificent evening. Only You know the cries of their hearts.

I pray You hear their prayers and answer them in Your time as you see fit.

I lift up those friends that know of You yet are scared of jumping in faith, leaping into Your arms. We as followers know You have a plan, but it's hard sometimes to understand why they can't leap. We walk in faith and know in time they will all be brought to You. Lord, by Your grace. Bless all of them whether they believe or not and until the sun shines again to give them peace and rest.

Allow them to somehow feel You pulling at their heartstrings because we know all too well how much You love all of us.

Amen.

THE LITTLE THINGS

LORD, ON THIS beautiful evening I praise You for all you've done and for all You are. I found so many reminders of your love today; tiny hummingbirds that fluttered in the sky singing a sweet song, serenading me. The rhythm of their wings is a true demonstration of how intricately everything is designed with perfection by You.

How grateful I am for your love and grace. Even something as tiny as the hummingbird flying above, His wings in constant harmony to your love song, is my constant reminder that You are here.

Selah.

BECAUSE OF YOU

MY LORD, MY lovely God, You take my breath away! I am awe-struck in what You are doing in my life. Tonight, the intimate moments I spend with you are immeasurably amazing.

You refuel my heart with love and allow me to look back on my life without tears, showing me only the good in my life. I am blessed!

Sometimes it's so hard to explain how I feel. Mere words aren't enough. It's mesmerizing that you have been here all along. Your love for me is beyond my comprehension. I am refueled by your grace. How I needed to just be still, to spend an intimate moment telling You how much I love You.

Knowing that You love me more than I can comprehend, fills my heart with joy. I will forever love You! You have given me friends that have opened up my heart. You breathed life back into me when I was gulping for air. I live, I breathe, because of You. Selah can't even describe how majestic You are in Your loving kind ways. I lift up my life to You. I live through You.

I am me, only because of You. I will shine for You! Amen.

REMAIN STILL

LORD, YOU SUSTAIN us by meeting all our needs. Even sometimes when we know not what we want, You have a way of filling tiny little voids in our hearts.

There are times when our anxious heart beats harder for you and we know and we ask that you come and fill us with a newness in You. You know the whys and the hows of our lives, we long for your embrace and gentle touch.

When we grow weary from a long week, help us to find peace and rest.

You know we seek solitude, yet our minds sometimes can't seem to find peace, help us to find it. In the darkness of the night when we awaken from a deep slumber, show us how to remain still. Let us hear your whispers, those faint callings of our name.

We draw closer to You. Wrap us in a loving embrace and rock us gently back to sleep, so we can rise in the morning and be refreshed.

Selah.

TOMORROW

May your tomorrows be filled with many blessings.

May you find the good in everything around you.

May God shine His light upon you and give you abundant grace and peace.

May He grant you the ability to see just how beautiful you truly are.

Take a chance, see yourself through His eyes. He sees the beauty in you.

He sees the ability for you to succeed at anything you put your mind to.

Let go, let God.

Such hope never disappoints or deludes or shames us, for God's love has been poured out in our hearts through the Holy Spirit Who has been given to us. Romans 5:5

THE GROWING SEASON

THE OWLS WILL hoot, and the midnight moon will shine a path leading you to where you need to be. Change is unique to each soul on this planet. No two life-changing moments are the same. Each life trip, each destiny quest into our future can only be predetermined and known by God. The deepest of moments, the tranquility of a shiny new evening, brought on by the glistening sleepy sun, can only show us that all we do and all we have, are our gifts in the moment, our brief moments in life.

Our own unique season of change can bring new dimensions in our thinking, new depths in our relationship with God. As the Earth comes to its midnight rest, as the sun sets and the moon glows, we are beckoned to listen to Gods calling, Gods truth. We need to be closer to Him.

Change can refuel our faith in God and bring us closer in our relationship with Him. He calls our name on the brief breezes of the day. In these tiny intimate moments in time, He will meet us and challenge us to change. He wants us to evolve into who He intended us to be, giant thinkers, deal breakers, God lovers. We are the ones to show the world our beloved Jesus. He calls us to our seasons of change. He calls us because He loves us.

SEASON OF OUR LIFE

LORD, BLESS US during this season of our life, You know the season of change and enduring more than we ever thought we could? How we love You, raise up our arms to You. It is You who is always there by our side. How magnificently stunning is your grace. We are in awe of your loving heart strings entwined in ours. You breathe into our lives the love of our eternal bliss, and we humble ourselves at your feet.

Nothing can stop our heart beats for your love. Fill us with compassion and kindness. Allow us to show others how You can fill their hearts to capacity with your love. Let them see You in us. Let them crave You through us. May we drink You in, and quench our thirst to the core of our soul, so we too may feel the green pastures of our life! Amen.

The Lord is my Strength and my Song, and He has become my Salvation; this is my God, and I will praise Him, my father's God, and I will exalt Him. Exodus 15:2

TEACH US TO DREAM

THANK YOU FOR this day Lord, it was a blessing. Although for some, today made them weary and worn, replenish their souls, Lord. Give those that are lost, the knowledge that they are growing.

Teach us to understand when we remain in your word, it will keep our heart in tune with You. Sing your sweet words of love to us Lord as we sweetly melt into dreamland. Keep our dreams joyful, show us how to dream of You and what You have in store for our lives. We live for You, Lord. Thank You for our blessings today.

Teach us to dream Lord, show us your multi-colored visions of our life. Teach us to dream, and to believe that with You, all things are possible. Teach us, Lord, to know that You are in control of our destiny, and what a beautiful destiny You have set before us.

In your sweet name,

Amen.

THESE DAYS

ON THIS SIMPLY stellar evening Lord, step into this night and fill our hearts with more love and mercy than we've ever known. Hearts are pounding in crisis. With every heartbeat, the hurt of the world resonates from forest to forest. Wash the pained hearts, Lord, like the waves rushing to the shorelines.

Engulf us with so much love that we surrender all that is. These moments of heartache, when there is war, hatred, and the times of not knowing what tomorrow will bring, makes us long for your tender touch.

Teach us to savor the moment Lord. Savor each and every moment of our lives, and to catch the essence of every breath our children breathe.

Help us to notice the moments, even the tiniest of moments, so we may indulge ourselves in joy, especially when our Earth is in such turmoil.

I shall not die but live, and shall declare the works and recount the illustrious acts of the Lord. Psalm 118: 17

ETCHED IN HIS HANDS

EVEN BEFORE YOU went to bed last night, before lunch and dinner, before that appointment, that meeting, even that special trip Jesus knew. He heard you call. and listens to every word you whisper, every song you sing. He hears you when you cry out to Him, He hears your voice. Nothing surprises Him, nothing will ever stop Him from loving you. He knew you before time began, your name is engraved on His hands.

Nothing will ever stop Him from loving you. Nothing will ever make Him stop watching over you, because in all this world, in all this entire land, He loves you and nothing you can do will change that. Make sure tonight you call – Call on Him for He's listening and waiting for your call. Call on Him - He's your Maker, your Deal Breaker. He's the one who holds your heart in His hand. He holds your life in His hands. He is the only one who understands.

Wait and hope for and expect the Lord; be brave and of good courage and let your heart be stout and enduring. Yes, wait for and hope for and expect the Lord. Psalm 27:14

THIS IS THE MOMENT

WHAT YOU MAKE of this moment, right here, right now is up to you! You can go it alone, which I promise is harder and more frustrating to do – or, you can call Him out! Call on Jesus, because friend, it's too hard to go it alone!

What if the path you choose is the long way around? Choose Him, and the path will be clear. It will be vividly breath-taking. It is worth the risk to call Him out. Don't turn around He'll call you back, even one hundred times until you listen, He'll call you.

What you make of this moment, right here, right now is up to you, it can change everything. This world, it comes with no instruction manual, no book of joy, hope or love. All these things come neatly packed in our hearts, just waiting for us to find them. Our children, family, and friends can sometimes leave us so drained, yet so loved. Jesus can refuel us. He revives us and makes us whole. When our family needs us, they need Jesus too. Show them the way, show them the love of Jesus.

Love - the unexplainable, fill up your soul, feeling that no one should ever have to do without. Love, the love of a parent, child or friend is just this, ultimately the divine, Our Jesus, drenching us with the purest feeling on the planet ... Jesus' Love. Seize these moments and call on Jesus – He's right here with you.

To the one only God, our Savior through Jesus Christ our Lord, be glory (splendor), majesty, might and dominion, and power and authority, before all time and now and forever (unto all the ages of eternity). Amen (so be it). Jude 1:25

INTIMATE MOMENTS

FATHER, I'M HOME. Thank You for this beautiful day. Lord, my heart is heavy, yet I know you're in control. Sometimes it's so hard to put it all in Your hands. I'm tired, I'm weary and I need You.

You have given me more in this lifetime than I could ever ask for.

I sit here alone, just wanting to spend an intimate moment with You.

How I love You! I am simply overwhelmed with emotions from your love, grace and your unending kindness. I could never, nor do I ever want to spend one intricate millisecond without You.

Thank You for your undying love and favor, but most of all, thank You for all the friends that You've placed in my life who pray with me, for me and my family who undoubtedly adore You the same. Grant us a restful evening tonight, Father, and may You wrap all of us in your blanket of protection. Amen.

MIND MOVIES

WE LIVE, WE laugh, we cry. Sometimes we are boastful and too wrapped up in life to even care. It's in these unexplainable moments in time that we take a memory, a mind movie from our memory bank and withdraw it, and play it for hours on end. It's in these moments we realize we indeed have it all. The family that loves you, children that adore you, friends that take your breath away with their devotion and love. Family and friends that pray with you and for you. It's a life given to us by our Almighty Father.

It's our life, and how we live it that determines who we are in Christ.

It's how we live our life, how we set the pace for all those watching, that determines how we walk as a faith follower.

Your life, my life, our life on this planet is set to the beat of God moments.

Little blessings, huge happenings and tiny falls to our Earth are what make up our day. How we rise, how we treat each moment is how we are defined.

How we bless others with our attitudes, good or bad is up to us. Free Will.

Give it all you've got. One shot, one life. Make it count for someone, anyone.

Be the "mind movie" that someone will play later. Be the memory for those, the memory that will make their heart smile. Be the Mind Movie Jesus would want us to be!

And all these blessings shall come upon you and overtake you if you heed the voice of the Lord your God. Deuteronomy 28:2

AHA MOMENT

FATHER, IT'S THE middle of the night. I need an aha moment. The moment between night and day, dawn and dusk where we know we will have enough strength to go on because of You.

My heart cracks open, and I implore You to fill me up with the good stuff.

The grace, mercy, and love from your eternal being, so I may shine again.

I am surrounded daily by those that need to be fed on your word. They are looking and seeking You in the corners of their heart. Help me, Father. Lead me, so I can help them find You. The view of the mountain from where I stand is massive, but I know I can climb it with You by my side. I continue to look up as I forge forward, chipping away at life, inch by inch. I know You wait for me at the top of this mountain in life.

Amen.

And let us not lose heart and grow weary and faint in acting nobly and doing right, for in due time and at the appointed season we shall reap, if we do not loosen and relax our courage and faint. Galatians 6: 9

TO FEEL GOD

IF YOU ASK me what it feels like to feel God, to be loved by God, and to know God, I'd tell you this … all the love of your family, children, loved ones and friends wrapped up together – this feeling, this love can't even compare.

It's the true belief, total trust and knowing and understanding that no matter what, your loved ones, your friends, are held in God's hands.

God, this being, this Savior is all I have, all I ever need. Almost indescribable, yet this love is the ultimate, take your breath away, sunset to sunrise, beautiful child and loved ones all rolled into one.

Father, Son, Holy Ghost, the ultimate without You, can't compare it, who would want to live life without this feeling, not I, love.

And the Lord answered, If you had faith (trust and confidence in God) even [so small] like a grain of mustard seed, you can say to this mulberry tree, Be pulled up by the roots, and be planted in the sea, and it would obey you. Luke 17: 6

CRAZY IN LOVE

LORD, ON THIS stellar starlit evening, we are just simply amazingly in love with You! We are crazy in love with your grace and blessings, and the way You always have the timing down to the precise minute to capture our weary, aching hearts. You seize our day with your lovely way of infusing our souls with love, and your intimate touch of kindness.

We find You in every cloud formation as the sun sizzles on the horizon. You reach for us, and like tiny children lost in a magical world of Legos, You find that perfect piece, that piece of your heart and make us swoon for You.

May your heart swoon for Him tonight. May you find Him in the corners of your heart and be mesmerized by His amazing love. May you become crazy in love with Him as He sets your heart on fire.

If I [can], speak in the tongues of men and [even] of angels, but have not love (that reasoning, intentional, spiritual devotion such as is inspired by God's love for and in us), I am only a noisy gong or a clanging cymbal. And if I have prophetic powers ("the gift of interpreting the divine will and purpose"), and understand all the secret truths and mysteries and possess all knowledge, and if I have [sufficient] faith so that I can remove mountains, but have not loved (God's love in me) I am nothing (a useless nobody). 1 Corinthians 13:1-2

GRANT US A NEW DAY

LORD, ONCE AGAIN it's raining. How I love the sound of rain falling, as its soft interlude of gentle beats helps to relax and calm at the end of the day. Darkness has fallen, and with You, I feel safe and secure. You are in my heart wrapped tightly in my soul for eternity. I can't imagine life without You.

Watch over my family and friends tonight, and let them feel the calming essence of the rain falling down tonight. Thank you, Father, for the abundant love You have shown all of us. Embrace all of us as we drift off to sleep.

Thank You for blessing me with the love of friends I couldn't imagine existed. Keep everyone happy, and give them a restful sleep tonight. Let us awaken to a new day of granting others the knowledge that they too can find peace and joy through you. We are relentless in our love for you Father.

Amen.

OUR LIFESAVER

AND NIGHTFALL COMES spiraling in with a dewy mist that engulfs even the most uncertain of things, we are drowning Lord, drowning in a pool of faults, pure doubt and we are trying to tread water lightly. We know deep in our souls these thoughts are not our own, none of it is true. Father as we swim in the abyss of unknowns, we get up on the high dive of our life. We want to jump in knowing without a doubt You are our lifesaver and we can always swim to You, for You will always save us. You have thrown us tons of ropes, but our self-centered ways make us swim into the abyss.

You seek us out like a lifeguard looking for the drowning soul. It is You Lord standing at every rim of crystal blue waiting on us to swim to the surface. It is You Lord who will save us from our own self-centered destruction. Kindness abounds and your love dives deep into our heart and soul, as we surface with outreached hands. We breathe You in like pure oxygen that allows us to inhale your beauty and on your embrace, You hold us in a lifesaving grasp. Lord, it is You, our healing God, may you remain in us always, giving us buoyancy to float through our days and help us to stay afloat, for we need You now more than ever in this sea called life.

Selah

HIS PROMISE

REMEMBER HIS PROMISE "there is more to come"! More beautiful than you can imagine, more peaceful than you can imagine. More of Him than you can ever dream possible. He's in you. Seek more of him and He will show you doors opening and others closing, and in the here and now, and the tomorrow's of our life more will become your "normal" as you grow more in love with Him!

Draw closer, read His love notes in the word – Soon you will know, He wants nothing more than for you to love Him, for He loves you more than your heart can hold. His love for you is endless. Nothing more, nothing less, He loves you!

Because your loving-kindness is better than life, my lips shall praise you. So will I bless You while I live; I will lift up my hands in Your name. My whole being shall be satisfied as with marrow and fatness; and my mouth shall praise You with joyful lips. Psalm 63:3-5

BEAUTIFUL YOU

CONSIDER THIS BEFORE you consider everything else; nothing would be the same if you didn't exist! Every place you have been, every heart you have touched, everyone you have ever spoken to would not be the same without you.

We are all connected by a common thread that points to Heaven. We are all affected by the decisions and even by the existence of those around us –

We are all touched by God who thinks you are amazingly beautiful! So, never doubt, never underestimate how important you are in God's ultimate plan. You have made so many lives better, every heart rejoices that knows you.

For He foreordained us (destined us, planned in love for us) to be adopted (revealed) as His own children through Jesus Christ, in accordance with the purpose of His will [because it pleased Him and was His kind intent]. Ephesians 1:5

YOU SAY YOU CAN'T? I SAY YOU CAN!

A SIMPLE REMINDER that you are you here for a reason. No one else can be you, so get busy! Show everyone what you've got. Throw out "the shoulda's", the "could haves" and start being who you really, truly want to be... You.

The old you or the new improved you, either way, no matter what - no one can ever take you away from you.

They can throw insults and words that hurt, but if you repel the words, and don't allow them to penetrate your heart, you can bounce. You can find "you" in the remote part of your soul hiding and just waiting for "you" to come get "you".

Today's the day. Everyone is waiting on you, you that you've forgotten about. So get out there!

Everyone is waiting on you! The beautiful you, who is known and loved.

You have been regenerated (born again), not from a mortal origin (seed, sperm), but from one that is immortal by the ever living and lasting Word of God. 1 Peter 1:23

WHO IS JESUS?

JESUS IS MY Lord and Savior. To some, that may be true, but truly who is He to you? To me, He died on the Cross and set me free. By the blood He shed, everything that makes me who I am, what I've done and all my wrong doings to everyone who I've crossed paths with are forgiven. I no longer walk with the guilt and shame of who I was - I now walk with Jesus in me, with me and all around me in the beauty of the night and day. He is the ever loving, unstoppable being that by faith alone, I know without a doubt lives in me and through me. His Grace has been given to me, and because of this, I want everyone to know Him.

His love is unending and when you ask Him to come into your heart, slowly your life changes for the best of the best. You no longer go through a day alone. You can speak to Him anytime and He is there waiting, listening and ultimately working in my life every millisecond of my day and night.

I shall engage in conversation with God to live and learn His ways. I will keep studying the bible so I can get to know our Savior inside and out. Conversations and faith keep us going. Miracles happen every day! From tiny God nudges to the ultimate life changing God moments, simply live your life in constant motion for Jesus. It's no longer about me! My Life is completely and undeniably about Him.

Little children, let us not love [merely] in theory or in speech but in deed and in truth (in practice and in sincerity). 1 John 3:18

SYMPTOMS OF HAVING GOD IN YOUR HEART

1. You are forgiven.
2. Life just keeps getting better
3. The sermons at church get better and better
4. You no longer get mad, you are happy
5. You suddenly forgive and let go
6. You look up a lot
7. You constantly smile
8. Instead of worry you give it up and pray
9. You look forward to sharing the word of God
10. You will receive grace from the almighty Father above
11. Suddenly having a man in your life takes on a whole new meaning.
12. You are overwhelmingly Joyful.

But none of these things move me; neither do I esteem my life dear to myself, if only I may finish my course with joy and the ministry which I have obtained from [which was entrusted to me by] the Lord Jesus, faithfully to attest to the good news (Gospel) of God's Grace (His unmerited favor, spiritual blessings, and mercy). Acts 20:24

ACHING HEARTS - LETTER FROM GOD

TO THE ACHING hearts that so many want to mend.

Be still and know I hold your heart in the palm of my hand.

You ache, I ache.

I know the road is hard, I know you miss what was. I know you want it all back. I know you want a do over.

For those that miss those who are no longer here, their time was short, but I am with you, waiting for you to give your heartache to me.

For those who choose to go it on your own, I'll wait.

I will carry your burdens, like dozens of grocery bags you carry into your homes. I wait for you to call on me, but you are too busy trying to do it all on your own. When you are ready, your destiny awaits!

Your life can be transformed through me. I wait. I sit by your side keeping you safe. Know that with me you will never be alone. All of the burdens of your life will be lifted. I will carry you forward, I will mend your aching heart.

Cast your burden on the Lord [releasing the weight of it] and He will sustain you; He will never allow the [consistently] righteous to be moved (made to slip, fall or fail). Psalm 55:22

CIRCUMSTANCES OF LIFE

LORD, SOMETIMES THE circumstances of our life take us away from our comfort zones. Help us to rely on You for strength. Give us the ability to keep our enemies far away.

Stay close to our hearts Lord, and help to guard our hearts against all the wrong thoughts and desires. Help us to stay in the moment with You.

Help us to realize when we work diligently for You, our comfort level cannot stay the same.

Help us to remain and see the beauty in the moment.

Allow us to find comfort in knowing You are here protecting us, holding our hearts and blessing us with the power to have the strength to remain still in You.

We live for You, Jesus!

Make today our best day, show us Your plan for our lives.

Let them see You through us.

Help us to endure the circumstances of our life!

Help us to remain steadfast in You.

Amen.

A BETTER WORLD

LORD, HERE WE sit waiting for your voice to echo through the evening breezes.

The softness of the wind slowly carries our thoughts away, and we embrace the quietness of the moment. Bless and comfort those who are hurting.

Literally torn up inside by moments, moments that no one should ever have to endure.

They await your final call to glory, and they seek your guidance.

Some are dealing with issues that most should never know.

The heartache of a messed up world still in progress.

The lost, the homeless still seeking your guidance and comfort.

Show them, allow them to feel your presence and know, that You are sending them someone who will give them the guidance and the words. Hope to help the hurting, the ones that are dealing with the pain of families in turmoil.

Show them that their hope is Jesus.

Guide them to your light.

Grant them gentle slumber and the knowledge that tomorrow will come, and be better than any today.

This is your world, make it a better world. This is their world, made better by You. Melt into their hearts, show them a world made better, by You. Amen.

PLANTING SEEDS

It takes only a kind word,

to plant a seed in a tiny soul.

May you someday see this soul

blossom and grow into someone you know,

who was once someone you knew all along

had the potential to be who they could be.

Water with kindness,

watch the garden come alive.

Shine God's light!

[For I always pray to] the God of our Lord Jesus Christ, the Father of glory, that He may grant you a spirit of wisdom and revelation [of insight into mysteries and secrets] in the [deep and intimate] knowledge of Him. Ephesians 1:17

JOY

I WOKE THIS morning and found "joy" tucked neatly under my pillow, and I placed it in my heart! It was seeping out from under my pillow like a giant cotton ball you tuck in a box that is too small. All puffy and light, joy struck me this morning and I'm keeping it and spreading it around. Joy is like a piece of bread with holes in it, you can't keep the jam from seeping through. You can't keep joy to yourself, you have to spread it around! If you find joy, catch it! If you have joy spread it around!

Joy for the taking, pick it up, tuck it into your heart and spread it around!

Be thankful for all you have and all you are. Raise your hands up to Jesus and thank Him for your home, you family and for your warm bed. Thank Him for who you have become, and who you are becoming because of Jesus.

We are all changing daily, and our circumstances can make us great, not ungrateful! Don't let your circumstances hinder who you were born to become … one grateful, joyously struck, awesome Christ child.

Up to this time you have not asked a [single] thing in My name [as "presenting all that I AM]; but now ask and keep on asking and you will receive, so that your joy (gladness, delight) may be full and complete. John 16:24

LIVE LIFE.

LIVE YOUR DREAMS. Be joyously proud, happy and thankful all in one day.

Be humbled, because Jesus shed His blood to save us all, and we are indeed forgiven. His plans for your life are amazingly beautiful.

Let us then fearlessly and confidently and boldly draw near to the throne of Grace (the throne of God's unmerited favor to us sinners), that we may receive mercy [for our failures] and find Grace to help in good time for every need [appropriate help and well-timed help, coming just when we need it]. Hebrews 4:16

QUIET MOMENTS

SO HERE'S THE thing, tonight as the tree frogs amp up their song in tune to the crickets chirping, know this day is over and done! The weary and leery can be assured that doing "your heartfelt best today" didn't go unnoticed. The kids may be trying hard to test your patience, but deep down inside they know you'll always have their back and the hard things in life won't always be so hard. Just comfort and hug on them, just love them. Today is a memory and be assured you get another do-over tomorrow filled with a great big dose of grace. Messy grace and the dishes didn't get done, and the littles running around will love you and bring you joy tomorrow.

Tip toe in and watch over them sleeping. Say one-thousand praises for this day. Maybe today didn't turn out as you wanted, but it turned out that you gave it your all. Send praises up for all the blessings in your life, big or small. The more you praise, the louder the Angels sing. As the tree frogs and crickets amp up their melodies this evening, feel blessed for all you are and have in your life. There is a symphony playing in the night sky, but the real symphony of love is playing in your heart. You gave it your best today. You gave today your all and the symphony playing, is your heartbeat beating in rhythm to Gods playing "I Love You" back and forth all night long.

Feel His touch of Mercy tonight as He tucks us all in knowing, we are His beloved and we wouldn't want it any other way. You are loved by God – Rise tomorrow knowing it's your gift to open slowly, savor the day and every moment.

Take time to ground yourself with Jesus truest blessings! Spend some quiet time with Him at Sonrise or Sonset – Drink in the beauty – Set the quiet tone in your life – Spend an intimate moment with Jesus. He is your Jesus, He is your King, and He longs for an intimate conversation with you.

"Who by [Your] might have founded the mountains, being girded with power. Who still the roaring of the seas, the roaring of their waves, and the tumult of the peoples. So that those who dwell in earth's farthest parts are afraid of [natures] signs of Your presence. You make the places where morning and evening have birth to shout for joy. Psalm 65:6-8

DELIGHT AND EMBRACE

MAY YOU GIVE thanks for all the blessings God has given you. May you delight in knowing how much He loves you, and may this love remind you to hope in Him. You are so special to God. May He grant you safe travels to and from your destinations every day. May your heart be touched, exactly the way you've touched so many people already. God is amazing and He just plain loves, no added blah, blah, blah. It's just that simple! Soak it up for a moment, it is real – He loves you without end.

Enjoy every day and allow others to know how much you care about them. We all need to know how much God loves us because you never know, we might be in Heaven tomorrow! God is coming for us, we don't know when, but all you have to do is love Him back. It's really that easy.

There is so much unknown in our daily lives. Unknown futures, unknown tomorrows, but one thing is sure ... Crucifixion Friday came and so did Resurrection Sunday. He died. He was raised, He lives forever.

Because He died, we can face tonight and tomorrow, and all the rest of the unknowns. All our fear can disappear because we know He holds our future. Life is beautiful – because He lives!

Because if you acknowledge and confess with your lips that Jesus is Lord and in your heart believe adhere to, trust in, and rely on the truth) that God raised Him from the dead, you will be saved. Romans 10:9

RUNNING HARD

WHEN YOU GET to the middle of your week remember this, the high hurdle in the middle of the week can be surpassed by You - the greatest of runners! Now let's make it one short stride to the end. Hand off the baton of grace to everyone that passes you by does your wrong or even right. It's time to set the pace to run to the end. Breath is coming in quick gulps as you swallow down that oxygen, breathe in grace and exhale those thoughts of discontent. This life is made for champions, and you are a champion of God's grace. He's molding you into a winner to run against the enemy, know you'll win every time because God is right there running with you.

It's time to throw down those thoughts of discontent and become content with Jesus, for He's the "Golden Trophy". He's the reason we race daily, for we race to His arms to ultimately slow down our day and find peace. We run to God, we run to Him and praise Him for this dear life!

In You, O Lord, do I put my trust and seek refuge; let me never be put to shame or [have hope in You] disappointed; deliver me in Your righteousness! Bow down Your ear to me, deliver me speedily! Be my Rock of refuge, a strong fortress to save me! Psalm 31:1-2

THE PROMISE

Remember His promise, "there is more to come."

More beautiful than you can ever imagine.

More peaceful than you could ever know.

More of Him than you could ever dream possible.

He's in you, draw nearer to Him. He will show you doors opening and others closing. In the here and now and the tomorrow's of your life, more will become your "normal" as you grow more in love with Jesus. Draw closer, read His love notes in His word – soon you will know, He wants nothing more than for you to immerse yourself in His love.

His love for you is endless.

Nothing more, nothing less, He loves you!

I love those who love me, and those who seek me early and diligently shall find me. Proverbs 8:17

MY BELOVED, (NOTES FROM GOD)

THE BATTLE IS never easy, the victory is everlasting if it is fought for my glory. Don't give up on your faith when you grow weary from struggling through life. I have an endless supply of grace to get you through the pain, ridicule, and problems in life. You will lose, only if you forget I am fighting for you. You will have many days when the wind will blow, just like when the enemy strikes blowing you down and you feel you can't get back up. The victory is not measured by how you feel or what you win or lose; it is indeed measured by your witnessing in the midst of warfare - when you win souls for my kingdom. Your strength will be renewed when you focus on fighting for what is right in my sight. Now is not the time to give in or give up, it is time to get on your knees and let me reveal to you what is worth fighting for.

But no weapon that is formed against you shall prosper, and every tongue that shall rise against you shall how to be in the wrong. This [peace, righteousness, security, triumph over opposition] is the heritage of the servants of the Lord [those in whom the ideal servant of the Lord is reproduced]; this is the righteousness or the vindication which they obtained from Me [this is that which I impart to them as their justification], says the Lord. Isaiah 54:17

BELIEVE IN YOURSELF

GOD KNOWS YOU are pushing through. He knows you're pushing through the week, days of doubt, and minutes of daunting tasks, He knows your every move. He has ordered abundant GRACE for you this week. Draw closer to Him, His strength will help you get through all the hard things.

Say this to yourself over and over ... "I am deeply loved, divinely appointed, abundantly equipped and cherished by God. No plan of Satan or obstacle can keep me from God's highest and best will for my life.

As I follow the voice of my Jesus, I can see the invisible, accomplish the impossible. I am a living, breathing miracle because Jesus Christ lives in me!"

For the Grace of God (His unmerited favor and blessing) has come forward (appeared) for the deliverance from sin and the eternal salvation for all mankind. It has trained us to reject and renounce all ungodliness (irreligion) and worldly (passionate) desires, to live discreet (temperate, self-controlled), upright, devout (spiritually whole) lives in this present world. Titus 2:11-12

BECOME SONDRENCHED

MAY THE PHRASE "Let go and let God" take on a whole new meaning for you. May you learn to rest while He works on your behalf.

May you understand your life journey and do only what He tells you to do.

May you live free from worry of others opinions, so you're free to love others the way Christ does.

May others be so drawn to your heart filled with the love of Jesus, that they come to know Jesus for themselves - because of you.

May you become Son drenched, as He whispers your name.

FAITH

SHE WALKED OUTSIDE feeling her way down the steps until she felt the road under her feet. Desperately she listened for the crunch of the tiny pebbles as she put one foot in front of the other, but the pebbles were gone and the road was smooth. Stunned, she stood there unsure which way to go. She heard a whisper "follow me". She reached out and felt His hand grasp hers. She said, "I can't find my way". He took her hand and put it on His shoulder and softly said: "I am the way, follow me". "I am your eyes, walk with me". She took a step and only heard silence, and in that moment she heard Him say, "I picked up all the broken pieces, you can walk free".

In that moment she knew her trail of brokenness was no longer her path to follow, for He had her. Her Savior had cleared the path of her brokenness, and all she had to do was follow Him.

Examine and test and evaluate your own selves to see whether you are holding to your faith and showing the proper fruits of it. Test and prove yourselves [not Christ]. Do you not yourselves realize and know [thoroughly by an ever increasing experience] that Jesus Christ is in you – unless you are [counterfeits] disapproved on trial and rejected? 2 Corinthians 13:5

LETTERS FROM GOD

I AM YOUR night and day, your Alpha and Omega. Fear is a thing of your past. I give you grace, ultimate confidence and the sheer knowledge that you are mine, and I have you!

Come to me, wrap your finger around mine like you did as a child. I will lead you to Eden. I will take you by the still waters and restore your soul. Breathe in this day knowing, all that is and was is not yours to keep for you are not from this world, you are heaven made, heaven sent. Let go and let me lead.

The stars that shine, all of those that shine so bright are people you will meet. Acquaintances, old and new, friends, and these stars that shine, all of those that shine so bright, are indeed the people you will meet on your journey through life. These stars they go on without end! You are made to guide those to be spirit driven, spirit filled, as I have filled you with my love. Guide those, show those how enchantingly beautiful their world can be, when they call Me into their heart.

I am your world, I watch over you. Know I will never leave you.

LOVE LETTER FROM GOD

MY FAITHFUL SERVANT and friend, if I could give you the answers for all your prayers I would. Some are not in the here and now, remain patient. I have such great plans for your life. Be still in the moment and know that I am there alongside you as you learn and trust who I am, and how I can transform our life.

I adore your faithfulness and your kindness that trickles into every heart you touch. You are so worthy of all that is good.

As long as the sun sets in the west, I will always love you, you are my faithful servant who lives for me.

1000 PRAYERS AND PRAISES

SO, WE COME on bended knees Lord, for we are not done, and when we are not done - we know You are just beginning! We tether a rope onto You, for You'll get us through. We will never entertain thoughts of leaving your side, because You are our deal breaker and we made a deal with You the day we laid it all down - the day You walked right into our hearts. Our names are etched on your heart and we know you've got this, because You made a deal of a lifetime when you crawled up on that cross for us, and You took on our sins as we became your forgiven children. And although we don't deserve this grace, and such a beautiful love, we send up 1000 praises for our lives, Your Son Jesus, and everything that is anything in our lives. Then the prayers come on stronger and longer, for nothing can stop the soothing words that come from our heart and flow into You. You are our Alpha and Omega, our only God, our King and tonight we lift up the unspoken prayers and we ask You to listen with a bended ear. Our children are offering up healing prayers, praises and we are filling the heavens with our love and devotion. Praying is the ultimate language we speak, and no matter how it is spoken, we speak our words of love to You. May 1000 prayers and praises shake the heavens tonight as we lift up our heartfelt words to you.

Selah and may You fill us with peace as we lay our heads down tonight.

I AM

I AM WITH you on a dark, dreary night when your soul is crying out to me.

I AM the fire that burns so bright inside of you, and if you would only leap to the next level of what I have in store for you, you'd know, you'd know I AM.

I AM the one who's there when you cry out in anguish, "Why don't you save my world"?

I AM the true love in your heart. I AM the smile on your child's face, the hug of a friend, your everlasting love.

I AM here on all the days you are longing for something more.

I AM JOY!

I AM LOVE!

I AM!

Fear not, [there is nothing to fear], for I am with you; do not look around you in terror and be dismayed, for I am your God. I will strengthen and harden you to difficulties, yes, I will. Isaiah 41:10.

CRACKS IN YOUR HEART

AND WHEN YOU stand still long enough to realize, this bruised soul inside of you just needs a tiny bit more light, you lay it all down in front of Him - cracked heart and all. He steps in and lifts you up, and as He does, He sends you extra helpings of the good stuff – through the cracks in your heart. Your heart seals up so the joy doesn't dare leak out! For as He sends you tiny morsels of love and heaps on multiple doses of grace, you can only think about all the times this week He truly picked you up. The times between kids screaming, the rushing here and there to the appointments that seem to never end. It's in these tiny moments where you thought you were busted to the seams with weariness, you realize you really aren't busted at all. He's giving you second and third helpings of His love, and the refreshing water He's using to quench your dry bones, and He revives you.

After this beautiful love feast, where His love is so bountiful He assures your heart He's right here and has been all along, you can say nothing but "All is well with my soul." Sink into the easy chair for the day, put up your feet and breathe Him in knowing you are so loved by Him, nothing can take you down. He's been there all along holding you up. He moves through you and around you; after all, He's your Savior and He always saves the day!

The Lord appeared from of old to me [Israel], saying, Yes, I have loved you with an everlasting love; therefore with loving-kindness have I drawn you and continued My faithfulness to you. Jeremiah 31:3

RUMBLING FAITH

THE TREES ROCK to and fro in rhythm to the wind. The soft breezes beckon fall to come. Fall, a season of welcomed change, and a time to plant seeds in other people's lives around you.

Being bold in faith takes a faith that rumbles like the wind – in tune to the sun as it settles in for its night rest. And as the moon peeks through the trees, its translucent beauty reminds us, there is always light to be found in the darkness.

Set your world in motion – This world needs hope and it needs to know, we find hope in Him. This world resonates a fire in her belly, a fire only Jesus can light to bring this world to its knees, to bring her peace.

Light the world up – Spread the word – Jesus is alive in you, and your hope is in Him.

And as the evening comes to the great mountains shout "I AM," for He is our Alpha and Omega, our night and day – and tomorrow shall ring out with His love and devotion.

But you are a chosen race, a royal priesthood, a dedicated nation, [God's] own "purchased, special people, that you may set forth the wonderful deeds and display the virtues and perfections of Him Who called you out of darkness into His marvelous light. 1 Peter 2:9

GOD'S HUSH

IN THE QUIET of the evening, just as darkness starts to settle in for the night, there is this God breathed hush that can take your breath away. You feel grace move on in like a blanket of thick fog, and it's your reminder of just how loved you are. God, He's just so good as He encircles your home, and the quiet of the evening just breathes His desire for you to draw closer.

Breathe Him in and realize that this day, this day is coming to an end and God is granting you a peaceful sleep. Embrace this day and all that was knowing you gave it your all, and all of it is God breathed. There amongst the softness of the evening, God is stepping in and saying "you, my lovely, have graced this Earth, and all is well with the world tonight". Know that everything in your life is a gift, and God is here waiting for you to allow Him to calm your mind and soul and feel His love embrace you.

And like a warm blanket of protection, your heart can embrace a calm; allow your lips to whisper to Him "I love you," and all is shall be well within you.

For we walk by faith [we regulate our lives and conduct ourselves by our conviction or belief respecting man's relationship to God and divine things, with trust and holy fervor; thus we walk] not by sight or appearance 2 Corinthians 5:7

Rest well, knowing He's right there by your side, and all is well with your heart and soul.

26 GIFTS

SO, MAYBE TODAY didn't go as planned, or maybe today was just "another day in paradise". Either way, you have potential – you are stunningly equipped by God! Need a reminder?

26 amazing gifts He sees in you:

You are:

Awesome	Brave
Content	Daring
Exceptional	Fabulous
Generous	Happy
Inspiring	Joyful
Kind	Loved
Magnificent	Noble
Optimistic	Passionate
Quaint	Radiant
Stunning	Thankful
Unafraid	Victorious
Wonderfully Made	Xenial
You are loved	Zestful

Another day in paradise? With Him, anything is possible! Seize your day!

FATHER

You are my strength, my daily input of placing all my days' struggles down. I unpack my baggage at your feet.

I know, I am sure You are my heart song. You are my only desire. In You, I find oceans of sanctuary.

Help my heart to stop aching, for it was singing all day. Teach me to place the little things, the minuscule moments that although bothersome, place them to rest. These moments, these heart-stealing, joy robbing moments and memories I leave with You. I'm done picking them up over and over. I know You can wash these moments out of my soul, for I only want it to contain You.

Forgive me for even entertaining these thoughts for a moment. I'm trying, and learning. It's all for You, for You are all I want and need. I seek You out and call your name. I hear You speak and I listen, for your words are the sweetest melody to my heart.

Selah

FROZEN WONDER

HAVE YOU EVER noticed how the ice on trees glistens in the moonlight, almost as if God's golden fingertips of light, are majestically painting the trees? Have you ever listened to the ice crunching under your feet, only to realize that God's path next to yours was silent, simply because He was carrying you with the lightness of Grace? Have you ever wondered on a beautiful glasslike, icy, stormy evening how every one of God's people makes it to the next day? For some, enduring life's most difficult storms, the most heart-wrenching problems?

God is working miracles everywhere you look. From the smallest of things to the largest. He's working His love line through the universe. Go outside for a brief moment and take in His beauty. Breathe in His world that by His Grace, glistens with frozen wonder, on a frosty evening. This evening is filled with His love and admiration for all of us to see. Feel and breathe Him in.

To Him be glory in the church and in Christ Jesus throughout all generations forever and ever. Amen (so be it). Ephesians 3:21

RAINDROPS

IN THE STILLNESS of the evening, you can hear the beauty of raindrops falling. As each drop falls, and you can hear God speak the words we desperately need to hear. Each drop brings a majestic calmness to our day, as He whispers words that drench our dry bones.

"MY BELOVED"

"LOVELY,"

"BEAUTIFUL,"

"FORGIVEN,"

"MY CHILD FULL OF GRACE,"

and you want desperately to shout to the heavens, "You are my Lord and Savior". How I love You.

Sweet songs of the evening as raindrops dance, and you can feel His presence in the storm. Draw nearer, call Him closer as night falls around your world. How we love His majesty, our Lord, and Savior of our world.

Men will say, Surely there is a reward for the [uncompromisingly] righteous; surely there is a God Who judges on the earth. Psalm 58:11

THE STORM

THE SKY LIT up and it is brilliant! White lightning reminding us of who we are in Christ, so small yet held in His arms during our storms in life. There is strength in the clouds, in God and a storm is coming to drench our parched world with life-giving rain.

One by one the drops come; one, two, three than more, and our world is alive with a symphony of rain falling and thunder cracking through the night sky.

God is beckoning our attention and He is listening to the thousands upon thousands of prayers being lifted up.

The growing season is upon us, and with it brings a newness in us through Him.

Embrace it. Find your place in the world with Him.

Rejoice in the Lord, O you [uncompromisingly] righteous [you upright in right standing with God]; for praise is becoming and appropriate for those who are upright [in heart]. Give thanks to the Lord with the lyre; sing praises to Him with the harp of ten strings. Sing to Him a new song; play skillfully [on the strings] with a loud and joyful sound. Psalm 33:1-3

RIGHT HERE RIGHT NOW

WHERE ARE YOU going in your life? What are you doing, while this world we live in spins out of control?

What you make of this moment, right here, right now is up to you.

You can run with the players that would rather hate than love, or you can just love. It's a scary world, but remember you can go it alone, which I promise is harder and more frustrating to do – Or, you can call Him out!

Call on Jesus, because friend, it's too hard to go it alone! What if the path you choose is the long way around? Choose Him, and the path will be very clear. It will be vividly breathtaking. It is worth every risk to call Him out, even when you grow weary don't leave His side. Don't turn around for He'll call you back. Even one hundred times, He'll call on you until you listen He'll call you back.

What you make of this moment, right here, right now is up to you. It can change everything.

The Lord is good, a Strength and Stronghold in the day of trouble; He knows (recognizes, has knowledge of, and understands) those who take refuge and trust in Him. Nahum 1:7

VICTORY SONG

THE DEVIL WILL show himself in many ways. He knows your weaknesses. He knows all your flaws. He knows your wishes and your wants. He will bring you those that are unsure, those that will make you question, "is he right?" Is she telling me the truth"? You'll question everything.

Think with the mind of the spirit and stop thinking with the mind of the flesh. Listen to the mind of the Holy Spirit. Be led with your heart, not with your mind, even if it doesn't make any sense, don't question God's intentions.

Follow your heart, your Jesus' heart. Jesus will lead you and you might question, but have faith and keep going. Jesus will ask you to follow, go. Don't hesitate – Your destiny is in Jesus' hands, not yours, only His! Pray without ceasing. Walk in the word of God. Fight for the life Jesus gave you, fight for victory because you are worth it! Our mind and attitude must be renewed daily. Set your mind for victory. Set your mind to knowing you are worth it. Allow yourself to find joy in Him and you will find it. Make up your mind that you will have everything that Jesus died for you to have. Shake off the wishbone and get a back bone! Make up your mind to live a joyous life through Jesus and then you can truly sing the victory song.

I have set the Lord continually before me; because He is at my right hand, I shall not be moved. Psalm 16:8

YOUR WILL BE DONE

WE LIFT OUR cares, our troubles, and our personal thoughts to You, Lord. May the wind whisk our countless cares away on pillow like clouds. Grant us a gentle peace as we lay me down to sleep. We lift our entire world up to you Lord, hear our prayers – the loud ones bellowing out for your help tonight, and hear the whispers of the unspoken prayers all whisked away on gentle breezes, as the heavenly angels sing.

Watch over our world, may your will be done.

We love you Lord and we thank you for your faithfulness. May our world peacefully come to rest tonight, and may your words penetrate the hearts of those who have heard them. May they shout your name to the mountaintops for all to hear. Keep our hearts in constant motion with You, and may we know to the depths of our souls that You are in control, Your will be done.

Amen.

FALLING FROM GRACE

FOR I HAD fallen, and You lifted me up. I felt your breeze of beauty as I looked into your eyes and I saw a love so deep – I saw You!

You place your gentle hands on my face and kiss my cheek with your lips of gold. You are my love, my Heavenly Father, You are my Lord!

You have lifted me from the dark abyss, You light my way to my future dreams. You know my needs, my cares. When I wander, You call, for it is You who draws me back. I long for more of You. May I drink You in like a crystal blue sea drenching me on a summer day. May I become Sondrenched and find You looking in my eyes with a love so deep, I no longer search, for your love fills me up and my heart is full.

Amen.

NATURE'S WONDER

IN THE SERENITY of the evening darkness, the world comes alive with the chatter of crickets calling in unison to the world. The cricket song is requesting sleep for one and all. Tree frogs singing and Gods small creatures are calling out to Him one by one, singing their love song in harmony. This evening is an enchanting reminder of God's love for all of us.

Off in the distance beyond the woods, the hoot owl is calling loud and clear "Jesus Come, our Jesus come." The hoot owl knows what the world needs; gentle rock-a-bye's from Jesus' embrace, and the brilliant wonder of His love echoing from the tiny creatures who never stop serenading Him all night long. The Earth is calling to God, and His gentle whispers echo through the trees, "Be still and know I am your God, be still and know I am". This gentle reminder calms the earth as Jesus draws nearer to us, on this enchanting evening which can only be orchestrated by Him.

Rest well and know your God is with you and all is well with your soul.

Selah

For ask now the animals, and they will teach you [that God does not deal with His creatures according to their character]; ask the birds of the air, and they will tell you; Or speak to the earth [with its other forms of life], and it will teach you; and the fish of the sea will declare [this truth] to you. Who [is blind as] not to recognize in all these [that good and evil are promiscuously scattered throughout nature and human life] that it is God's hand which does it [and God's way]? In His hand is the life of every living thing and the breath of all mankind. Job 12:7-10

BUSTING THROUGH

LORD, TODAY YOU and I busted through the busy. Without You, I am nothing. The world spins and tonight when I thought I was drowning, gulping for air - You came in like a soft breeze, like pure oxygen quenching my lungs. I got lost in your sky. Breathless was the night sky as I looked up for answers, and as I paused and whispered "Selah," You, my Lord, my El Shaddai rescued me from drowning in my crazy day.

What had I missed? Do we as God's treasured ones, the ones who endure a crazy paced life of shuffling kids here and there, working and keeping our homes in order; do we live as if we enjoy and search for the presence of God in our daily lives? Do others see Him through us? Have we allowed the precious gift of God at work in our lives to go unnoticed? Have we forgotten all that He is and can do in our lives? Have we allowed this precious gift of His mercy and grace to slip through our fingers, in all our busyness?

Lord, we want to live with the expectancy of You moving in our lives – help us to breathe You in, and on the exhale find peace and joy through You.

In You Yahweh, we find peace.

And behold, I am with you and will keep (watch over you with care, take notice of) you wherever you may go, and I will bring you back to this land; for I will not leave you until I have done all of which I have told you. Genesis 28:15

ALWAYS PRAY AND REMEMBER

HERE'S A LITTLE reminder as you unwind from your day...

Look up He's shining like the Sun. How quickly our thoughts can turn away when all we have to do is turn to Him. Fall undeniably in love with Jesus whose heart beats with yours.

Silence trickles in at the end of the day. Hear His whispers of love and allow yourself to be Sondrenched by Him. Breathe in and on the exhale bask in His glory. He's breathing love and peace into you. Let go of today's troubles, because His supply of love and peace is endless.

As the day quiets, exhale His love and send it to the highest mountains so the world can feel this great love in the glow of the sunset.

This is a gentle nudge to remember the subtle reminders of how desperately we need to feel Jesus' love. Always pray and remember, He is the first and only love of our life.

Selah

GOD'S HEARTSTRINGS-LOVE NOTES FROM GOD

I STEPPED OUTSIDE and in the chill and fog You Lord caught my eye. As the three-quarter moon shown down so bright, it was almost as if You were winking at the world and I heard you say,

"In this imperfect world, it is impossible to be perfect! There will always be mistakes and errors for the time, but in my eyes, you will always be mine. Forgive those who have wronged you, just let it go. For it is in the releasing of your hearts greatest weeping you shall find me. In these tired days where you are trying to do it all, as the heart wanders away from me, consumed by this great race called life, I will call you. I see beauty in you, a beauty that only I can see. Be kind to yourself and those around you, for everyone has their own weight to bear. The greatest challenge I ask of you is to remain with me and allow me to remain with you. These days are not as long as you feel, let me take the burden from you. You will feel a great release."

May you feel your heart strings entwine with mine, and as the moon as big as the sky watches over the world, it is I watching and keeping in time with the Son. My love for you will never end, for as the moon greets the Son at dusk, it is I greeting you, shining my light ever so bright. Whisper my name – Jesus, for I am always right here."

Sondrenched Holidays

May the joy you find during the holidays be
with you all year long.

PRAYER FOR A NEW YEAR

LORD, CALM OUR hearts for this longing, this desperate need to know what the New Year will bring and what lies ahead on our journey into the future. Sustain us and help us to maintain the simple truth that You have us, and yes it will be okay.

When our road gets curvy, rocky or takes a wrong or different turn, draw us back in, back into your loving arms.

Keep our eyes fixed on You Lord, as we look up seeking your truths and grace. May we see your tiny love notes in everyone and everything around us. Send us gentle nudges to remain still, slow down our hurried lives and have faith in knowing everything will be okay, because You are in control.

May we bless others to the fullest, as our presence resonates your love in their minds, leading those who are lost back home to You.

Keep us passionately engaged in your word, and may You hold us tightly in your arms as You rock us to and fro.

May You have your will in our lives in the New Year to come.

Your will your way, always.

Amen.

IF GOD SENT VALENTINE'S

IF GOD SENT Valentine's would the Post Office be so overwhelmed that they'd have to shut down? Would there be so many Valentine's that they'd spill out into the streets, and clog traffic for months to come? Would there be red hearts blowing around in the wind on a trail of love that would become endless and never stop, until time ceased to exist?

God sent His greatest Valentine many years ago. God sent His Son to save us all. Every day, every minute, every second of life can be Valentine's Day, because God resides in our hearts. You are loved!

For God so greatly loved and dearly prized the world that He [even] gave up His only begotten unique) Son, so that whoever believes in trusts in, clings to, relies on) Him shall not perish (come to destruction, be lost) but have eternal (everlasting) life. John 3:16

There is no greater love. God's love is endless, timeless, it's everlasting!

APRIL FOOLS'

THERE IS NO April fools' joke when it comes to Jesus. No pranks, no lies, no false hopes – just truth. He loves and is love.

Today is your new day and it's filled with possibilities.

Let those around you - see you. No Joke! Let those around you see who you really are - spirit filled and driven by Him.

Let your light so shine before men that they may see your "moral excellence and your praiseworthy, noble and good deeds and recognize and honor and praise and glorify your Father Who is in Heaven. Matthew 5:16

HOLY THURSDAY

JESUS SAT THERE and shared the Last Supper knowing His disciples, His friends would turn their backs on Him. What loneliness, what hurt, what ultimate pain.

What great love Jesus had to have to die for us. There is none greater, and therefore He left His final commandment,

I give you a new commandment: that you should love one another. Just as I have loved you, so you too should love one another. John 13:34

You will never find a greater love because Jesus is the greatest love!

EASTER SUNDAY

IT'S WONDERFULLY MADE Easter Sunday and He has risen! Every detail of your essence is God-breathed. Find your soul drenching love in Him today. He's the one true King who laid it all down, was crucified, died and rose on this glorious Easter Sunday. There is no other God more brilliant or loving, there is no other God period.

Rise N shine you beautiful soul, don't give Satan a playground to say any different. Shout it out loud and clear...

"I AM HIS, HE LIVES IN ME, I AM A CHILD OF THE ONE TRUE KING. I AM HEAVEN BOUND, MY RESERVATION HAS BEEN MADE BY HIM."

Today is the day, feel His embrace – He loves you more than anyone could possibly love.

We give thanks to you Jesus, because of your sacrifice, we are washed whiter than snow, and we are amazingly and miraculously made.

HUG-O-WEEN

I DRIVE TO a neighborhood and listen to kid's laughter. Everyone, parents included, are walking down the street for Halloween and I think, "Why can't we have Hug-o-ween instead of Halloween?" A time when everyone just knocks on the door of the little ole lady handing out candy, you know the lady, the one we pass by all year, but not on this one night? Why can't there be Hug-o-ween where we knock and just say "hey you, yeah you, I care."

And my costume would be a chain of hearts, thousands of hearts around my neck, because simply that's how many hearts I want to touch- and when the little old lady stands in the street, I'd say, "Hey, do you know the Son that shines on your every day? He loves you, and He sent me to give you a hug and just say, how's your heart today?"

By this shall all [men] know that you are my disciples, if you love one another [if you keep on showing love among yourselves]. John 13:35

SLOW DOWN CHRISTMAS

I WANT TO slow down Christmas. I want to slow down the magic, slow the hustle and slow the timing until the day of Christmas arrives. I want to count down to Christmas but, not to anticipate presents; I want to anticipate the presence of Jesus in my life daily, every day and especially on Christmas day.

Why is it as we age, we seek a slowness, a softer approach to allowing Jesus to resonate in our souls? As we go year after year watching Christmas hasten in getting here, and the stores cram more and more Christmas spirit down our throats, Christmas has lost its wonder. I want my wonder back!

I want to resonate daily on how Mary and Joseph were so in tune with God, and how Mary trusted and had such great faith in our Heavenly Father. I want to always remember how she carried the Son of God, the Son of all mankind. I want to feel the emotion, the heartfelt love of this season slowly. I want to feel God.

I want to slow down Christmas and enjoy and feel the bliss in knowing this Son, this baby Jesus was sent for you and for me as I prepare for the arrival of our beloved Jesus in such a way, that this season means love, grace and a beauty like I've never felt before. I want to slow down Christmas and savor every moment of our Christ Child.

May you find Jesus in your heart and soul, and may His love for you be a constant reminder this Christmas season. May you feel His grace and may the Christ child touch you in such a way, that everyone around you wants to know who this Christ child is. May you whisper Sweet Jesus name and hear His breath in every thought and prayer you say. This Christmas may He become your Savior like never before, and may he be remembered all through the year. Hold onto this season and shine His love all year long.

Behold, the virgin shall become pregnant and give birth to a Son, and they shall call His name Emmanuel – which, when translated, means, God with us. Matthew 1:23

GOOD CHRISTMAS EVE

THE BEAUTIFUL CHRIST child awaits our celebration. Born to love us, and in our amazement no matter what our past holds, He loves us unconditionally.

His gifts are not extravagant like a shiny new car, but when it comes to love, He never stops giving.

I hope you have the Merriest of Christmases ever. My wish for you is peace and blessings that never cease to amaze you. We are so blessed by the Heavenly Father of love, hope, peace, joy and the list goes on and on. Make your list and check it twice, His love, hope, joy and peace are all you need.

The Christ child was born to love us and His promise of Eternal Life is the gift to share. Share His love this Christmas season so others feel it too

Glory to God in the highest [heaven], and on earth peace among men with whom He is well pleased ["men of goodwill, of His favor]. Luke 2:14

WHAT'S IN THE BOX?

IF YOU'VE EVER watched a child waiting for Christmas, you will without a doubt laugh and remember your childhood gone by. The anticipation is undeniably a butterfly, belly laugh filled day that encompasses thousands of questions about what is in the specific box. By the time they get to the ultimate opening of the gift, you are about as ready as you can be to see the expression on their face. You know that they have definitely run out of guesses, and you are plain worn out from answering questions. What's in the Box? Open the present! That was the dialogue on Christmas day!

When it all comes down to it, it's not about what's in the box, it's about what's in your heart. What has God placed there, and have you opened the present He placed there, day after day trying to get your attention? Open the Present! Tucked inside your heart is the presence of Jesus, the most beautiful gift of all seasons. It is indeed the presence of Jesus Christ, the tiny baby born so long ago on Christmas. He's waiting for you to open the Present, His gift of eternal life! Joy for the taking, what are you waiting for? Open the present and receive the greatest gift of your life. The presence of Jesus Christ tucked neatly inside your heart. Merry Christmas – Open the present.

But God's free gift is not at all to be compared to the trespass [His grace is out of all proportion to the fall of man]. For if many died through one man's falling away his lapse, his offense, much more profusely did God's grace and the free gift [that comes] through the undeserved favor of the one Man Jesus Christ abound and overflow to and for [the benefit of] many. Romans 5:15

THIS CHRISTMAS SEASON

ENTICE YOUR SENSES to feel and see the joy, the love and the empathy and favor from the tiny baby born in a manger. Imagine the world dripping with the love of our Heavenly Father, who sent His only Son to save the world.

Embrace this tiny baby Jesus and allow yourself to be wrapped in the timely feeling of unending blessings and joy. Find your favor, seek it out through the light of Jesus and enjoy this beautiful Christmas season.

Hold on to this Season of joy, knowing that with Jesus the best is yet to come. This season doesn't end at the stroke of midnight, this season goes on and on day after day and on into eternity.

For it is by free grace (God's unmerited favor) that you are saved (delivered from judgment and made partakers of Christ's salvation) through [your] faith. And this [salvation] is not of yourselves [of your own doing, it came not through your own striving], but it is the gift of God. Ephesians 2:8

HAPPY BIRTHDAY TO YOU!

YOU ARE A year older and wiser.

You can start this year with a clean slate and pursue your dreams.

Make a wish, say a prayer and make this your best year ever.

Count your blessings for you are indeed blessed.

Jesus Christ, your family, children, and friends love you.

God blessed the Earth the day you were born.

Every life you touch is changed by the imprint you leave behind. Leave giant imprints on everyone you meet.

May this birthday, this year be your best ever! May you find your joy in Jesus this year.

Happy Birthday in Christ!

I was cast upon You from my very birth; from my mother's womb You have been my God. Psalm 22:10

EPILOGUE

GOD'S PLAN, GOD'S will in your life … ask Him into your heart and watch your world unfold. If He's in your heart, reaffirm your faith, and become more in love with the Son of God.

Today is great!

Tomorrow with Him?

Astronomically fantastical!

Anything is possible with God in your heart.

Break the chains that hold you back … set yourself free.

On a Summer Day or any day, become Son Drenched.

Ask the Son of God into your heart.

May the God of your hope so fill you with all joy and peace and believing [through the experience of your faith] that by the power of the Holy Spirit you may abound and be overflowing bubbling over) with hope. Romans 15:13

NOTES

NOTES

NOTES

NOTES